THE NEW LONDON SCHOONERS.—The next SCHOONER from SYMON'S WHARF, Southwark, is intended to sail

On SATURDAY the 7th of March, 1829: And the Schooner A L E R T, now on her Passage, will leave Whitehaven, for Belfast and London, three Days after her arrival here.

For Freight or Passage (having excellent Accommodations) apply to J. H. and G. SCOVELL, Symon's Wharf, London; or

THOMAS HAMMOND, Whitehaven.

N.B. Shippers are requested to be particular in directing their Correspondents in London to forward Goods to Symon's Wharf, Southwark; and all Goods for the Country, or any of the adjacent Ports, will be forwarded without delay, with the greatest Care, and at the least possible Expense.

Whitehaven, 21st Feb., 1829.

The following additions to the Whitehaven Steam Company's Advertisment came to hand after our front page had been put to press:— "CONVEYANCE BY THE SAINT ANDREW, STEAM BOAT, TO CARLISLE ASSIZES:—At Five o'Clock on Monday morning, the 11th August next, the Steam Boat, St. Andrew, will sail from Whitehaven Canal Foot for Carlisle direct, calling off Workington and Maryport, for the purpose of taking Passengers. The Fly Boat on the Canal will be in readiness to take the Passengers forward to the City immediately on the arrival of the St. Andrew.—Magistrates, Solicitors, Jurors, Witnesses, and others having business at the Assizes, will find this by much the pleasantest, cheapest, and most expeditious means of accomplishing their Journey to Carlisle.—Should a sufficient Number of Passengers from the Assizes offer, the Saint Andrew will sail from the Canal Foot on Sunday the 17th of August, at Three o'Clock, for Whitehaven, calling off Maryport and Workington. The latter Voyage will offer an excellent Opportunity to Parties from Whitehaven desirous of viewing the beautiful Scenery on the Borders of the Solway.

Fares to the Canal Foot, Cabin 10s., Deck 5s.
Parties going up and returning the same voyage will be charged the above Fare only.
☞ The St. Andrew will Sail from this Port for Dublin on Friday Morning at Half-past Three o'Clock."

STEAM PACKET COMMUNICATION BETWEEN WHITEHAVEN AND BELFAST,

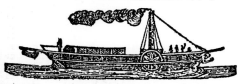

THE Steam Packet MAGDALENA is intended to sail for the Conveyance of Goods and Passengers from Belfast for Whitehaven

On Friday the 10th April, at Noon,
And from Whitehaven for Belfast

On Monday the 13th April, at 7 Evening.
The Magdalena will make at least one Voyage weekly between the Two ports.—Of the Days and Hours of sailing due Notice will be given.

For Freight or Passage apply to HILL CHARLEY, Belfast, or to

RANDLESON AND FORSTER.

Whitehaven, 30th March, 1829.

THE Steam Packet, Mona's Isle, leaves Whitehaven every TUESDAY, for the Isle of Man and Dublin.

Fares to the Isle of Man; Cabin, 7s. 6d., Deck, 5s.
Fares to Dublin; Cabin, 15s., Deck, 7s. 6d.

HOURS OF SAILING:—
Tuesday, July 30, Two o'clock Afternoon

AGENTS.
EDWARD MOORE, Douglas;
FISHER AND STEWARD, Whitehaven.

WHITEHAVEN STEAM NAVIGATION COMPANY.

ONE VOYAGE WEEKLY BETWEEN LIVERPOOL AND WHITEHAVEN.

THE Company's New and Powerful Steam Packet, EARL OF LONSDALE, will, during DECEMBER and JANUARY, perform One Voyage Weekly between LIVERPOOL and WHITEHAVEN, with Cargo and Passengers. To Sail from Whitehaven every THURSDAY, and from Liverpool every TUESDAY.

The following are the Hours fixed for Sailing.

FROM WHITEHAVEN FOR LIVERPOOL
FEBRUARY.

Thursday 4th Feb. ——	Midnight
Thursday 11th Feb. ——	Five o'Clock Evening
Thursday 18th Feb. ——	Midnight
Thursday 25th Feb. ——	Five o'Clock Evening

FROM LIVERPOOL FOR WHITEHAVEN.
FEBRUARY.

Tuesday 2nd Feb. ——	Eleven o'Clock Morning
Tuesday 9th Feb. ——	Three o'Clock Afternoon
Tuesday 16th Feb. ——	Eleven o'Clock Morning
Tuesday 23rd Feb. ——	Three o'Clock Afternoon

☞ *Shippers of Goods are requested to send to the respective offices, written notices of Shipments, specifying name of Shipper, Consignee, and Description of Packages, otherwise the Company will not hold themselves responsible in case of Loss, Delay, or Irregularity of Delivery.—The Company will not be responsible for loss arising in any way to Shippers of Stock, nor to Passengers for any loss arising to them by detention, or for lost luggage unless entered and paid for as cargo.*

Agent at Liverpool, WM. DOWSON, 8, Goree-Piazza,
FISHER & STEWARD, Agents, Whitehaven.

Whitehaven, January 30, 1836.

WHITEHAVEN HARBOUR

Aerial view of the Harbour, 1993, by Edward Clack.

WHITEHAVEN HARBOUR

Brian Scott-Hindson

Phillimore

1994

Published by
PHILLIMORE & CO. LTD.
Shopwyke Manor Barn, Chichester, Sussex

ISBN 0 85033 917 0

Printed and bound in Great Britain by
HILLMAN PRINTERS (FROME) LTD
Frome, Somerset

Contents

List of Illustrations

Author's Preface

This book is meant to mark the 100th anniversary of the creation of the Board of Commissioners of Whitehaven Harbour. However, the Board of Commissioners was preceded by the Board of Trustees of the Town and Harbour of Whitehaven and, consequently, the book is the story of the work of the almost two thousand men who served as Trustees or Commissioners over a period of almost three hundred years. Over that time they have been responsible for the development, building, maintenance and administration of the Harbour. Although paid no salary, they gave their time and worked for the benefit, as they saw it, of the Town and Harbour. They sometimes made mistakes, and were subjected to a great deal of abuse, particularly from the local press, when their decisions did not meet with popular approval. It is also the story of the owners of Whitehaven Estates and their relationship with the Trustees.

I wish to thank the many people who have helped me to compile this volume. Firstly, my grateful thanks to the Right Honourable the Earl of Lonsdale for writing the Foreword. I would like to mention Miss Anne Dick, Local Studies Librarian, the Daniel Hay Library, Whitehaven, who sought out books, documents and information over a long period of time. Similarly, I must thank Mr. Harry Fancy, Curator, Whitehaven Museum, who has supplied information and help along the way, and also Mr Ron Rigg, General Manager, Whitehaven Harbour Commission, for information regarding events during the 20th century.

The illustrations in the book were chosen from the museum's large and excellent collection of slides, photographs and illustrations. I am extremely grateful to Mr. Fancy for his help in choosing them, and also preparing them for publication, and for providing the captions.

Brian Scott-Hindson
St Bees, August 1994

Foreword by the Earl of Lonsdale

1994 marks the Centenary of the formation of the Board of Commissioners of Whitehaven Harbour—a body of Trustees responsible for the operation of the port, and also of the incorporation of the town itself as a borough.

Perhaps inevitable, a Centenary is the occasion for reviewing the activities of an organisation—what have been its achievements and what its failures during that period, and what are its prospects for the future.

The observant visitor to Whitehaven will quickly realise that the harbour is much too large for present-day needs. Its massive piers stretching defiantly into the waters of the Solway clearly represent a vast expenditure of capital, manpower and materials which can only have been justified by the former existence of a considerable fleet of vessels and firm trading links with other ports. In Mr Hindson's book, the creation of the port during the 17th century, its rise to international significance in the 18th, and its long, slow decline during the 19th and 20th are chronicled clearly, shrewdly and sometimes with humour.

Over a period of almost four hundred years, members of my family have been actively involved in the construction, operation and administration of the port, and in the early days of the development of the Town, of its businesses and its supporting industries; the Harbour of course was essential.

One hundred years ago, the management of the Harbour evolved into the Board of Commissioners, who are representative of users and investors and of the electors of local government, with four appointed by the founding Lowther family—persons of objective knowledge, skills and viewpoints to enhance the part the Harbour should, or could, play in the development and changing nature of the local economy.

I commend this book about Whitehaven Harbour, which is so inextricably linked with the Town and its hinterland, written by Brian Scott Hindson, now an author and lecturer of great knowledge, who came from his native Yorkshire in 1964, to follow his profession of accountancy with one of Whitehaven's foremost businesses (which he assisted to develop into a major North of England trading and service concern for the agricultural industry, which is my primary interest), and in his spare time he developed an interest in the history of the Town and district to the extent that he is now an acknowledged authority on the history of Whitehaven.

Lonsdale.

For
Pat, Penelope and Wendy

Introduction

The Town and Harbour of Whitehaven lie on the coast of West Cumbria on the principal headland between the Solway Firth and Morecambe Bay. Compared with many English towns, Whitehaven is of comparatively recent origin as, before the Dissolution of the Monasteries, Whitehaven was a tiny fishing village standing on land in the possession of the nearby priory of St Bees.

In 1600 part of this land was acquired by the Lowther family, and in 1630 it was conveyed to Sir John Lowther of Lowther in Westmorland, who purchased the title to the salt pans and coals in 1634/5. Sir John appointed his son, Sir Christopher, steward of the Whitehaven estate, and it is largely as a result of the initiative and effort of Sir Christopher, his son Sir John and grandson, Sir James, that by the middle of the 18th century Whitehaven had risen to become, after London, one of the six most important ports in the kingdom.

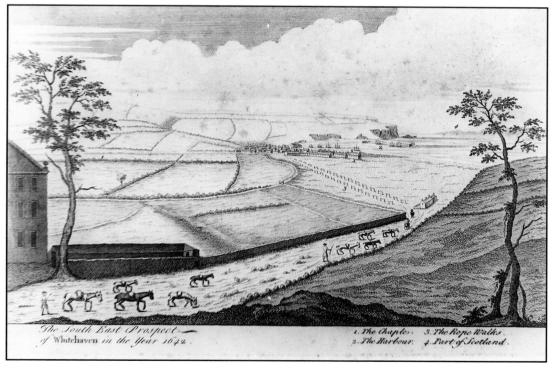

1 Prospect of Whitehaven, 1642.

1

Sir Christopher was aware that coal lay under his lands, and he began to develop these deposits, with a view to exploiting the ready market in Dublin, which was at the time the second largest town in great Britain. His first venture, however, was in the export of salt, and he built a small pier in the harbour in order to provide loading facilities and some protection for the vessels employed. Sir Christopher took up residence in Whitehaven in 1634 and then began the planned development of the town. It was laid out in a grid pattern, regular building plots were allocated, and strict building regulations were also specified. Thus began the development of the first planned town since medieval times.

Sir Christopher was made the first baronet of Whitehaven in 1642, but unfortunately he died in 1644 at the age of 33 years. His son, Sir John, was only one and a half years old at the time he inherited the title, and the estate was administered by trustees until he came of age. Then, in 1663, he initiated a major expansion of the town. He accelerated the development of the local coalfields, importing mining expertise from the Newcastle area, and he was also responsible for the settlement, encouragement and promotion of many kinds of commercial activity.

The Lowthers were absentee landlords. It is an odd fact that from 1634 to 1755, the years of direct supervision of the estate by the Lowthers, Christopher, John and James lived in their town for a total of no more than 25 years.

The Castle, Whitehaven.

2   Whitehaven Castle. The Whitehaven home of the Lowther family.

The estate was managed by a series of carefully chosen stewards. Sir John appointed first Thomas Tickell, who was estate steward from 1666 until 1692. Tickell was followed by William Gilpin, who held the position from 1693 until 1722. Sir James then appointed Richard Gilpin and John Spedding jointly. This last was an uneasy alliance, however, and Gilpin was driven out in 1730 by the greater efficiency of Spedding. All these men were of high calibre, and extremely able in their own right. Each played an important part in the development of Whitehaven, both as Lowther's stewards, and also in many commercial enterprises in which they became involved.

Both Sir John and Sir James were Members of Parliament for long periods, Sir John for more than 30 years, and Sir James for 55 years. Both worked tirelessly in Parliament in the interests of Cumberland and Whitehaven, and kept abreast of the latest developments in trade, technology and science. Both accumulated vast personal wealth. At the time of his death in 1755, Sir James was described as 'the richest commoner in the land', although during his lifetime he acquired the nick-name of 'Farthing Jimmy' because of his love of money.

Whitehaven lies on the Cumberland coal field, a small field of some 100 square miles, much of it lying under the Irish Sea. The coal is of excellent quality, and a substantial trade was developed with Dublin; many thousands of tons being exported annually. By 1730, the coal mines at Whitehaven were the deepest in the world. The Lowthers tried to gain a monopoly of the Irish coal trade, but failed because of competition from other local landowners, who began to exploit their coal measures, and also to develop the adjacent ports of Parton, Harrington, Workington and Maryport. The Lowthers did manage to gain the lion's share of the trade, however, due to their investment in the best available technology, and the appointment of excellent colliery stewards.

By the beginning of the 18th century, a significant new factor affected the local economy: the result of trade links with the New World. Merchants began to import tobacco from Virginia and Maryland in exchange for cargoes of manufactured goods. Important links were also established with the West Indies, whence sugar and spirits were imported. Several Whitehaven merchants were also involved in the slave trade, and some acquired their own estates across the Atlantic, setting up trading stations to facilitate the exchange of cargoes. As a result of the American War of Independence, Whitehaven lost its tobacco and slave trades as well as 100 ships, and its leading position as a port began to decline.

Over a period of many years, Whitehaven was of considerable importance in the shipbuilding industry. Its yards gained an enviable reputation for producing vessels of sound design and excellent workmanship.

Over 1,000 ships have been identified as having been built in the Whitehaven yards. Most of them were collier vessels of 150 to 250 tons, but larger vessels up to 3,000 tons were also built. The first shipbuilder of significance was Thomas Sibson (1686-1775).

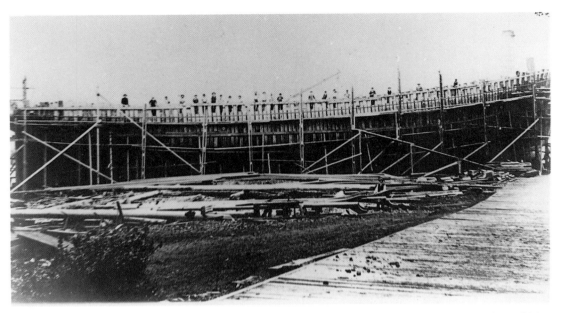

3 *Tenasserim* under construction at Whitehaven in 1861. This was the 161st vessel launched by the firm of T. & J. Brocklebank. She was 195 ft. long, with a beam of 35 ft. and a draught of 22 ft. She was of 1,002 registered tons.

William Palmer (1702-78) built some 10 vessels between 1757 and 1778. Perhaps the most interesting firm, however, was that of Daniel Brocklebank (1725-1801). He trained as a shipwright at Whitehaven, but emigrated to America in 1770, and established a shipbuilding yard at Sheepscut, Maine. At the outbreak of the War of American Independence, Brocklebank was fitting out the *Castor*. Deciding not to throw in his lot with the Americans, he returned to Whitehaven in this vessel, and again began to build ships, completing a further 27 vessels before his death in 1801. The firm was carried on by his sons Thomas and John until its closure in 1865, having built a total of 131 ships. At the end of the 18th century, there were five shipyards in operation at Whitehaven: Brocklebanks, Shepherds, Bowes, Nicholsons and Kirks. During the four years 1799 to 1802, these yards built 38 vessels with an aggregate tonnage of about 7,500. The majority of the ships were brigantines of 100 to 200 tons with some barques of 200 to 300 tons.

Conditions changed with the advent of the 19th century, particularly with the development of the East India trade, and there was a demand for larger vessels. About 1803, a partnership of William Wilson, Musgrave Walker and William Stitt began to build ships as big as 500 tons. The *Clarendon* (505 tons) was launched in 1807, and the *Earl of Lonsdale* (502 tons) in 1810. These were very large vessels for their day. Of the five yards mentioned, Brocklebanks worked until 1865, when the shipbuilding industry was in severe recession. Additionally, the firm was unable to

4 *Boyne* of Whitehaven. This 190-ton vessel was launched on 13 June 1794 by William Bowes of Whitehaven. This watercolour painting is one of only two known works by the artist William Jackson of Whitehaven. The picture is in Whitehaven Museum's collection.

renew its lease, as it was expected that the site would be required for a proposed wet dock. Shepherds ceased to build ships in 1803. The Nicholson yard closed in 1814, and the Bowes yard in 1831.

Another very important 19th-century firm was that of Lumley Kennedy and Company. Kennedy was a shipwright and manager of the Brocklebank yard for some 20 years. He left in 1835 and formed a company in partnership with Dr. Robinson, Bolton Hall: Mr. R. Jefferson, Springfield: Mr. H. Jefferson, Rothersyke: Captain Pew RN, Whitehaven: Captain I. Mounsey, Whitehaven: Mr. Thomas Beck, Whitehaven: and Mr. John Peile, Somerset House, Whitehaven. By the time of its closure in 1865, the firm had built 65 vessels, all of which were well known throughout the country for their sound workmanship and excellent sailing qualities. The largest, the *John O'Gaunt* (871 tons) was launched in 1855. The yard closed almost simultaneously with Brocklebanks, whose yard was taken over by the Whitehaven Shipbuilding Company,

5   The launch of the *Patterdale*. This 1,187-ton vessel was the first iron ship to be launched at Whitehaven. This illustration appeared in the *Graphic* magazine on 8 July 1871.

6   The 2929 *Alice A Leigh* being launched at Whitehaven in October 1889. She was the largest vessel ever built in the port, and also the next to last. Both she and the 2,374-ton *Englehorn*, launched later the same month stuck on the slipways, and had to be hauled into the water.

whose chairman was G. C. Bentinck, M.P. for Whitehaven. This company built several ships which were amongst the finest examples of the clipper ship era. These included the *Wasdale, Greta, Thirlmere, Rydalmere, Cassiope, Candida, Silverhow, Grasmere* and *Blengfell*. The company was forced into voluntary liquidation in 1879, but was reformed in the following year as the Whitehaven Shipbuilding Company No. 2. Again many fine ships were built including *Gilcrux, Dunboyne, Galgate, Lord Shaftesbury* (later *Golden Gate*), *Windermere, Englehorn* and the largest sailing ship ever built at Whitehaven, the *Alice A Leigh* (2,929 tons) in 1889. The *Dunboyne* is now preserved in Stockholm Harbour as the *Af Chapman*; the *Alice A Leigh* and the *Englehorn* both stuck on the slipways on launching, and they entered the water only after a great deal of difficulty and expense. The company failed in 1890, and the yard was sold in 1891 for £3,000, and for the next 10 years it was used as a repairing yard.

Part One

The 18th Century

Chapter 1

Acts of Parliament and the Building of the Harbour

Background

Before the end of the 17th century, Sir John Lowther was experiencing differences of opinion with the leading citizens of Whitehaven. For instance, many of the merchants and ships' captains wished to build their new houses along the Harbour side while Sir John specified that the best houses should occupy sites along the new streets, particularly Lowther Street, which he was laying out in the developing town. Also, there was a great deal of controversy about the building of a new church to replace the existing chapel which stood in Lowther Street at the end of Chapel Street. The chosen site for the new church was on a plot of land bounded by Lowther, Church, Duke and Queen Streets on which Sir John wished to erect a building aligned with the streets and designed in accordance with the best London practice. The people of Whitehaven, however, wanted the new church to be built aligned due west and east, and to a design of which they approved. In the event, and after considerable delay, a compromise was reached, and St Nicholas' church was built aligned with the streets, but to a locally approved design.

The main source of contention, however, concerned the development of the harbour. The Lowthers, who owned it, saw it as a facility to enable them to export coals, particularly to Ireland, where they already dominated the trade. Some of the town's merchants, on the other hand, were, by this time, trading with the American colonies and the West Indies and, because their ships were larger than the average coal boat, they needed deeper water in which to moor than was then available at Whitehaven.

Sir James, who inherited the Whitehaven estate from his father in 1706, was determined to gain a monopoly of the coal trade in the whole of west Cumberland, and consequently did not wish to become involved in expenditure which did not help towards that end. However, he was not opposed to the wishes of the merchants, and in 1708 he steered a Bill through the House of Commons which created a Board of Trustees which would control the future developments of the Harbour. He asked his agent John Spedding, 'I would know ... how the Town likes my willingness to give them any accommodation about the Harbour which they could hardly have obtained from my father'.

It is clear, though, from the way in which the 1708 Act was drafted, that Sir James did not envisage that his ultimate control of events would be in any way diminished. While he was prepared to provide a forum in which the leading citizens of Whitehaven could express their views on the various aspects of the development of the town and harbour, it would seem that he was more interested in finding a way by which the work on the harbour, urgently needed by the merchants, could be financed other than by providing the necessary money himself. In any case, he was careful to ensure that virtually all the provisions of the Act required his ultimate approval.

Before the Act of 1708, the leading citizens of Whitehaven had made several attempts to negotiate, first with Sir John and, after 1706, with Sir James Lowther, ways by which they could play a bigger part in the government of the town and Harbour.

The instrument used by the Lowthers for the running of the town was the Manorial Court Leet. However, the Court Leet had powers only to remedy wrongs, but was unable to propose and carry out desirable improvements. In due course, a group emerged, led by the Gale family, which demanded greater participation in town affairs.

The Lowthers saw the control of the Harbour as their prerogative, as before this date all expenditure had been made by them, and it had been built by them to suit their requirements. In any case it was their property. The aristocratic Sir John simply refused to consider any form of power sharing, but it must have seemed to many that Sir James was breaking with his father's policy when he apparently allowed control to pass into the hands of a Board of Trustees, as was provided in the Act of 1708.

The Act of 1708

Entitled 'An Act for preserving and enlarging the Harbour of Whitehaven, in the County of Cumberland', the Act of 1708 (7 Anne Cap 5) came into force on 25 March 1709 and is of major importance to the history of Whitehaven, as it formed the basis for all subsequent developments and extensions of both the town and of the harbour.

Firstly the Act describes 'The Bounds of the Harbour' as:

All that Precinct included within the Limits and Bounds hereinafter expressed, that is to say, beginning at the Wharf on the North-west end of Marlborough Street, and from thence in a Line North-east by North till the Middle of Lowther Street open upon it, and from thence in a straight Line parallel to the Range of the same street directly to the Low-water Mark; from thence by the Low-water Mark to the Rocks whereon the new Mole is begun to be erected, and so along the said Rocks by the Low-water Mark till it answer the Line of the said Mole; from thence along that Line till it come up to the said Mole, and so along the same Mole till it joyn upon the Old Pier at the Platform; and from thence, including the said Platform, along the new Wharf, till it meet with the Wharf of the West Strand near the House of Mary Addison Widow; from thence along the same wharf by the Custom House Quay in a straight Line to the West Side of the Timber Yard, and so along the Wall of the same Yard to the North West Corner thereof, and from thence by the North West Wall of the same Yard to the Wharf where it began.

A Board of Trustees 'of the Town and Harbour of Whitehaven' was then set up, providing: 'That James Lowther, Lord of the Manor of St. Bees for the Time being, and six other Persons be nominated, appointed and changed from Time to Time by James Lowther, his heirs and Assigns in Writing'. In fact Sir James always nominated seven rather than six, one of whom was to be his deputy at meetings at which he was not present himself. In this case the stand-in was John Spedding, the Whitehaven Colliery steward. The others were William Gilpin, John Ribton, John Golding, Anthony Benn, John Sheppard, and John Gilpin.

The Act also provided for 'fourteen other Persons to serve until the first Friday in August 1716'. They were: William Feryes, John Gale (Snr), John Gale (Jnr), Clement Nicholson, Thomas Coates, Peter Senhouse, Thomas Lutwidge, Richard Hodgson, Ebenezer Gale, Robert Blacklock, Robert Biglands, Christopher Dixon, Elisha Gale and Richard Filbeck. All these men were described in the Act as 'Merchants'.

In the event of the death or resignation of any of the 'fourteen others', the remainder were to co-opt any person they chose for the rest of the term. It was provided that 'On the first Friday in August 1716, fourteen persons were to be chosen by ballot', and that such an election was to be held every three years thereafter.

Apparently anyone could stand as an elective Trustee, as the Act does not specify any qualification or requirement for those aspiring to become Trustees. In practice, however, it is quite clear that each individual was required to be in a substantial way of some business which used the Harbour and, perhaps most importantly, also had to be acceptable to Sir James Lowther. The qualifications of those eligible to vote in an election of Trustees were clearly detailed, however. These were:

The Majority of the Inhabitants of the Town dealing by way of Merchandize in the Goods subjected to the Payments and Duties.
The Master of any Ship or Vessel belonging to the Port.
Those having a Part or Share of not less than one sixteenth in any Ship or Vessel belonging to the Port.

The form of franchise was not specified, but this method of electing the Trustees was subject to much abuse, particularly in the mid-19th century, when, for instance, young girls were provided with oranges to sell, thus enabling them to vote as 'persons dealing by way of Merchandise ...'.

Between 1709 and 1716, some replacements of the original elective Trustees inevitably had taken place. At the first election in 1716, all the survivors and those co-opted in the interim were re-elected.

Duties of the Trustees as Imposed by the Act of 1708

The harbour works to be undertaken as a result of the Act included 'the Completion and Finishing the New Mole aforesaid, and to make a Counter Mole and Head on the North East side of the Harbour, to strengthen and repair the Pier with a new Bulwark, other Works, and to cleanse and deepen the said Harbour'.

Prior to the 1708 Act, work such as the New Mole was financed by monies borrowed on the personal guarantees of some of the merchants, and repaid from 'accustomed Duties of Anchorage' levied by the Lowthers for the use of the Harbour. Under the new Act, 'the Duties are hereby wholly and for ever taken away and discharged', and a new set of rates and duties became payable from 25 March 1709 for a period of 14 years. The new duties were to be charged on the tonnage of coals exported, on the value of goods imported, and on the tonnages of ships entering the harbour.

The duty levied on coals was 'One Halfpenny for every Ton, computing One hundred and ninety two Gallons Winchester Measure to the Ton' delivered and put on board any vessel for exportation. The duty was payable by the ship's master before the vessel left the harbour, and he was permitted to discount the amount of the duty from the price of the coals.

The list of imported goods on which duties were payable was shown as:

For every Hogshead of Tobacco   Threepence
For every Hogshead of Sugar   Sixpence

7   Whitehaven Harbour tokens 1600-50. It is believed that these brass tokens were issued to the masters of vessels as proof that they had paid their harbour dues. The tokens are in Whitehaven Museum's collection.

For every Ton (per Tun of 252 gallons) Brandy or other Exciseable Liquors	Two Shillings
For every Ton of Flax or Hemp	One Shilling and Sixpence
For every Hundred of Deals	Eight Pence
For every Last of Pitch or Tar	Eight Pence
For every Ton of Iron	Twelve Pence
For every Ton of Raft or other Timber	Four Pence
For every Barrel of Herrings	One Penny
For every Pack of Linen containing Two Hundred Weight, computing One Hundred and Twelve Pounds to the Hundred	One Shilling
For all other Goods and Merchandize	Two Pence in every Twenty Shillings of the Value, as rated at the Customs House.

These duties were payable by the importing merchants.

Duties levied on the tonnage of the ships entering the Harbour depended on the ships' immediately preceding port of discharge:

If from any Port in Great Britain or Ireland	Two Pence per Ton.
If from any Port in Europe	Four Pence per Ton.
If from any Port in Asia, Africa or America	Eight Pence per Ton.

The said Tonnage to be admeasured as is described in an Act of Parliament made in the Fifth and Sixth Years of the Reign of the late King William and Queen Mary intitled 'An Act for granting their Majesties several Rates and Duties upon Tonnage and Vessels, and upon Beer, Ale and other Liquors, for securing certain Recompences and Advantages in the said Act mentioned, to such Persons as shall voluntarily advance the sum of Fifteen hundred thousand Pounds, towards carrying on the War against France.

All of the duties mentioned were payable for a period of 14 years, 1709 to 1723, during which time it was considered that sufficient money would be raised to pay for the works described in the Act. At the end of the period, two-thirds of the duties, the temporary duties, ceased to be payable, but the remaining third, the permanent duties, continued in perpetuity to pay for repairing, cleansing and general upkeep of the Harbour.

Because the Trustees were aware that the duties would not raise money at the same rate at which expenditure occurred, they were empowered 'by Deed indented under their Hand and Seal to convey and assure all the said Duties ... to any Person willing to lend at Interest not exceeding 6% per annum'. Those people holding bonds issued prior to the Act were invited to apply for the new ones and in the following two years bonds were issued to a total value of £1,970. Of this amount Sir James Lowther subscribed £500. Whitehaven Harbour Bonds were quickly seen to be an attractive investment opportunity. Once issued they changed hands several times, and at the end of the lending period, very few were repaid to the original investor.

Apart from overseeing the work on the Harbour, the Trustees were required to order and direct the collection, receipt and disposal of the sums of money raised from duties and expended on the Harbour improvements and were to present accounts on the first Friday in June every year. To assist them, any 11 or more Trustees were empowered to appoint a collector and to fix his duties and remuneration, at no more than 12 pence in the pound of the amount collected. The first monies received were to be used to pay the expenses of obtaining the Act. These amounted to £116 16s. 9d. in addition to 25 guineas paid for drafting and engrossing copies of the same.

The Trustees were also to appoint a pier master at a salary not to exceed £20 per annum. Peter Senhouse was the first chosen. The Act also contained a clause allowing the Trustees to appoint a 'scavenger' to ensure the harbour was kept clear and to levy a rate to cover the cost. There were also provisions for:

The preventing and Removing of all Annoyances from the said Town.
The orderly Cleansing and Paving the Streets of the Town.
The making of Sewers.

Why these matters were included is a matter of speculation as almost no action was taken, and the appointment of a scavenger later provoked considerable disagreement between Lowther and the Court Leet.

Each provision of the Act indicates the size of the majority of the Trustees necessary before anything could be done. For instance, any 11 Trustees could appoint the pier master, whereas Sir James and 15 others were needed to appoint the scavenger. Most importantly, any alteration to the Act required the approval of Sir James and 17 other Trustees.

The Act of 1711

It was noted in 1711 that 'as the Temporary Duties given by the said Act [of 1708], especially under the Discouragement of Trade during the Time of War, will not raise such sums of Money within the Term as are necessary for the Purpose aforesaid', the Trustees agreed to petition Parliament for a new Act in order to continue the duties for a further period.

In fact the financial situation had deteriorated to the point where workmen remained unpaid, and materials obtained had not been paid for. In this situation, Sir James agreed to provide £50 for each £100 raised by the Trustees, Sir James being content to lend upon the security of the Act whereas the Trustees were required to provide personal guarantees for money borrowed by them. With these conditions, the

Trustees raised £300, Sir James lent £150, and advanced a further £100 in order to provide a total of £550, a sum urgently needed.

Consequently an Act (10 Anne Cap 3) was obtained in 1711, which extended the period during which the temporary duties were payable for a further 14 years, that is until 25 March 1737. Under this Act, any 11 Trustees could approve the borrowing of the further sum of £1,350 'to be repaid in addition to amounts borrowed under 7 Anne and remaining unpaid'. Again interest was fixed at six per cent per annum.

Work began in 1709 on the building of the specified Counter Mole projecting into the Harbour opposite the end of Lowther Street, and continued until 1711. In July of that year the Trustees decided that the Counter Mole in that position 'will be too great a Confinement to the Shipping', and with the approval of Sir James decided to dismantle the work already completed and to rebuild the mole opposite the end of Duke Street, re-using the stones and other materials. In 1711, Duke Street had not yet been formed and the new site was described as 'leading to the Bridge at the North East end of King Street'. At the time, Plumblands Beck ran open down the middle of what became Duke Street and bridges provided crossing points.

Over the next few years, matters proceeded much more smoothly for Whitehaven Harbour. The Counter Mole or Bulwark was completed in the revised position and a deal of work was done to extend the New Pier. Trade improved and the Harbour became increasingly busy.

The financial position of the Trustees also improved until in 1716 they were able to cancel all 40 issued bonds and reissue them with interest reduced to five per cent. Further, in 1718, they felt able to repay all investors who were unwilling to renew at four per cent. By 1722, there were £1,530 of the Harbour Bonds outstanding, of which £1,230 had been borrowed since the passing of the Act of 1711. Because of the limit laid down in the Act, the Trustees were able to borrow only a further £120, and a bond in payment for repairs carried out following gale damage was drawn in favour of Sir James. Lowther undertook to continue his own bonds at four per cent interest and to pay off all the other bonds, 'so that the Growing Duties may be applied to the Works and Repairs of the Harbour'.

The Scavenger and the Court Leet

In accordance with the 1708 Act, the Trustees appointed a scavenger 'for the more effectual preventing the throwing of Ashes and other Annoyances into the Harbour'. A rate of 6d. in the pound was duly levied on property to cover the costs involved. The Trustees had even provided 'Publick Privies on the Beck near the Custom House, and near Henry Nicholson's at the South End of the Counter Mole over Plumblands Beck'.

At first this was opposed by members of the Jury of the Court Leet on the grounds that this aspect of town management was their prerogative. The Court Leet, however, having no powers, was in the unfortunate position of having to petition the Lord of the Manor, Sir James Lowther, in order to effect any improvements. Lowther did nothing to solve the matter, and allowed the division of authority to continue for many years.

However, in 1717 a faction of the Jury of the Court Leet, led by Ebenezer Gale, passed a verdict that 'We the Jury of this present Leet do look upon ourselves as Superceeded by the said Act [of 1708], and consequently not Obliged to Intermeddle in the matter of Nusanses Relating to the Streets, being now more properly the Business of a Scavenger, to be appointed, directed and ordered by the said Mr Lowther and the Trustees as the said Act requires'. A codicil was added to this verdict on the insistence of William Gilpin: 'and whereas we find any Nusanses in the Streets and Market Place, we Recommend it to the Trustees above mentioned to see to the due Execution of their Several good Orders made for the Purposes aforesaid'.

It will be noticed that both Gale and Gilpin were also members of the Board of Trustees. The Gale family, Virginia Merchants, held a powerful position in Whitehaven, and in 1716 no fewer than five members of this family were serving as Trustees. Gilpin was also in a powerful position; indeed he was Lowther's estate steward.

Sir James saw this as an attack by the merchants on his position in town government. He was quite right in that Gale and his colleagues, by attempting to transfer business from the Court Leet to the Board of Trustees, were trying to introduce a little democracy into the debate. Lowther, needless to say, was not prepared to be coerced into any form of power sharing, and made his position clear by 'packing' the next Court Leet jury, who were instructed to rescind the 1717 verdict, though in this he was unsuccessful.

1719 was an election year for the Trustees, and again three members of the Gale family were elected. Shortly after the election, the Board formally undertook to keep the streets of the town and the market place clean and tidy. They also advertised for 'Persons that are willing to undertake to clean Pow Beck from the South End of James Street downwards'.

In the following year, Sir James obtained an order from Kings Bench which enabled him to enforce the dismissal of two co-opted Trustees. He also accused the Trustees of not following the requirements of the 1708 Act sufficiently closely. Further, in 1721, following storm damage to the pier in the Harbour, Sir James gave his instructions regarding the repairs to John Spedding, and ignored the Trustees.

It should be pointed out that, at this time, the west Cumberland coal trade was severely depressed and, worse, it was thought that the Howgill mines were almost worked out. Lowther considered moving away from Whitehaven, having made enquiries about affairs at Maryport, and also at Saltcoats in Ayrshire. To say the least, he was disillusioned with the state of his affairs, and also of his relationship with the people of the town. In 1717 Sir James wrote a stinging attack on their attitude towards him in the form of 'An Advice to those that come to my Estate'—a memorandum to his senior employees.

> Trust not the people of Whitehaven, but expect all the returns that Ingratitude and Malice can invent. A few designing men to set themselves at the head of numbers will always suggest grievances and under the pretence of oppression lead them to do everything to thwart those so very much above them. All Services, all Kindness and Benefactions will be forgotten as soon as done and they will often do themselves an injury to do you a very great one. They served my Father so continually, who was their Founder, their Patron and constant Benefactor. They continually treated me so that took great pains to serve them. They grudged me the necessary improvement that attended the laying out of my own money, though they shared in the benefits. However, cease not to do them good, if not for their sakes, yet for the sake of God Almighty and your own.

Sir James, of course, was in a position to have his way, and at the election of Trustees in 1722 ensured that only those who favoured his views were 'elected'. Of the 14 Trustees elected in 1719, only one survived, while John, Ebenezer and Matthias Gale were all removed. Having thus reduced the opposition, Lowther then instructed the new Board to rescind the 1719 decision regarding the scavenger, a decision which handed back to the Court Leet the responsibility for keeping clean the streets of the town.

Lowther had gained a victory, but it was only a temporary one. The management of the affairs of the town was totally ineffective, and again the matter of the scavenger became a serious issue. The Court Leet was completely unable to keep the streets clean and tidy, and the Trustees inserted a clause in the Act of 1739 which again gave them powers to appoint a scavenger. This they implemented in 1744, thus precipitating a repeat of the earlier dispute. The ubiquitous John Spedding, however, ensured that orders were passed by the Jury of the Court Leet relating to the upkeep of the streets, while at the same time saw to it that the Trustees appointed and controlled the scavenger. Direct confrontation between Lowther and the Trustees was avoided, but again it was only a temporary respite.

The Harbour became so busy that in 1732, the Trustees thought it necessary that a new mole or wharf should be built and it was agreed to build the Tongue or Merchants' Quay. This was completed in 1734 and at the June accounts meeting in that year, John Spedding, the treasurer, presented the following account of monies due to Sir James Lowther in respect of the new Tongue:

Owing for money paid by Sir James for workmen	494	17	9
Owing to Sir James for money paid to Sundry Persons for wages and materials	346	1	7
	840	19	4
Amount paid out of Fund (duties)	260	0	0
	580	19	4
Interest on money due to Sir James	11	5	7
	£592	4	11

At this time it is clear that all work being carried out in the Harbour was being financed in the first instance by Sir James Lowther, repayments being made periodically from the accumulated duties. This was necessary as the Trustees had already exhausted their borrowing powers as provided in the Act of 1711. By 1736, Lowther was owed £773 and there were bonds unpaid of £220, a total debt of almost £1,000. It was calculated that the temporary duties, which were due to expire on 25 March 1737, would raise £400 in excess of running costs between September 1736 and March 1737 and that, therefore, there would be a deficiency of some £600 if the debts were to be repaid in full.

The Trustees were unwilling to go to the expense of a further Act of Parliament, and it was agreed that an attempt be made to continue the temporary duties by voluntary agreement with the coal owners, ships' masters, and ship owners. Sir James Lowther agreed to the continuation of the halfpenny per ton duty on coals exported, and undertook not to sell coals to ships' masters until they had paid the full tonnage duty. It was also agreed that duty received under this arrangement would be paid into a separate account, 'the Voluntary Fund'. Of course, perpetual duties were to continue as provided in the Act.

However, on 18 September 1739, one of the more important meetings of Trustees was held. Mr. Spedding produced accounts from 27 March 1737, the date on which the temporary duties ceased to apply, to various dates in 1739 as follows:

Incomes:-			
½d. per ton on Coals 25.3.37. to 24.6.39.	269	13	6
Tonnage duty collected 25.3.37. to 13.8.39.	542	16	1
	812	9	7
Perpetual Duties Colld 25.3.37. to 24.6.39.	369	3	4
	£1181	12	11
Harbour Costs:-			
Repairs—25 March 1737 to 25 March 1738.	200	19	2
Repairs—25 March 1738 to 25 March 1739.	164	2	10
Repairs—25 March 1739 to 15 August 1739.	105	18	10
Collector's Remn £1181.12.11. @ 12d per £.	59	1	8

Pier Master's Salary 25.3.37. to 24.6.39. @ £20 pa.	45	0	0
Allowance for registering accounts: 2 years	10	0	0
Total Disbursements	585	2	6
Total Duties (above)	1181	12	11
Balance in Treasurer's Hands	£596	10	5

The treasurer was ordered to pay to Sir James Lowther £593 3s. 0d. which was the actual amount due to him at 25 March 1737.

It was noted on 18 September 1739 that there were only three bonds still outstanding, two for the governors of St Bees School and one for Sir James totalling together £220. The Trustees also owed to Sir James £718 17s. 8d. for work which he had financed from March 1737 to September 1739.

At this September 1739 meeting it was stated that 'Despite the work done on the Harbour, Shipping has increased to such a degree that the Harbour is now too Scanty [sic] for the ships wanting to use the Harbour'. A long list of necessary work was also produced. This included 'the making of another Mole at a proper distance behind the present Pier for the reception of a few of the largest Ships when loaden'. It was argued that with the current debts no large scale expenditure could be undertaken because of inadequate income.

Once again, as in the early years of the century, the Harbour of Whitehaven was proving to be inadequate for the demands of the shipping wishing to use it. At that time, about one hundred ships were involved in the coal trade with Ireland and, in 1739, 36 ships arrived from Virginia and Maryland carrying tobacco. Again, the trans-atlantic merchants were demanding deeper water in which to moor their vessels.

The Act of 1739

Sir James and the Trustees therefore applied for a new Act of Parliament for an extension of the period of temporary duties. The new Act was that of 1739 (13 Geo 2 Cap 14), of which only four clauses dealt with Harbour matters:

The provisions of the two preceding Acts were to continue.

The right to charge temporary duties was granted for a further term of 21 years from 10 April 1740, with the right to increase the permanent duties from a third to a half of the appropriate rate.

The first duties received were to be used to discharge the total debts of £938 17s. 8d.

Such new works as were deemed necessary (none were specified) were to be undertaken, and the deepening of the Harbour and the maintenance of existing wharfs, bulwarks and so on were to be continued.

Clauses 5 to 32 of the Act dealt with the setting up of the Whitehaven Turnpike Trust. Although important, study of this subject is without the scope of this work.

By the late 1740s, many people were again thinking in terms of increased powers for the Trustees in matters affecting the government of the town. At the time, a scheme for supplying fresh water to the town was being examined, as was Carlisle Spedding's scheme to light the town using methane gas piped from the coal mines. Even Sir James Lowther agreed that, in the event of these matters coming to fruition, the Trustees would need greater powers.

However, a dispute over Harbour developments caused these matters to be shelved. During the decade 1740 to 1750, Whitehaven's tobacco trade had expanded at a phenomenal rate. In 1745, John Spedding described the trade as 'the very life and soul of Whitehaven'. 10.6 million pounds of tobacco were imported in 1748, a quantity which required some 70 vessels to transport, while by 1759 no fewer than 140 were needed. Over twenty ships each year were trading with the Baltic area, bringing timber, flax and iron for the local industries. The coal trade continued to expand and in some years, John Spedding, in his capacity as Lowther's agent, experienced some difficulty in obtaining a sufficient number of ships for the Dublin voyages. In the circumstances, the tobacco merchants in particular were no longer prepared to accept Lowther's dictates about Harbour developments, and while everyone agreed that the Harbour

8   Old Quay showing the watch tower and a building which was once a public house, and also provided accommodation for the Harbour Master and stores.

needed to be extended, Lowther wanted to lengthen the existing quays to accommodate more coal ships, whereas the merchants favoured the creation of an outer harbour, where the deeper waters would allow their bigger ships to enter at low tide. The result was a struggle between James Lowther and a faction led by Walter Lutwidge, an important overseas merchant and a Trustee.

The Lowther scheme for adding 30 yards to the Old Pier and building a new Tongue 'could not be carried into Execution for want of the full number of Trustees subscribing thereto required by the Act of Parliament, in spite of urgent Necessity, several Memorials and Petitions etc. Yet some few of the Trustees refused their consent to what was desired and which was approved by a great majority of the Trustees'. This was the situation in June 1751, and the matter was resolved at the election of Trustees in August 1752, when Sir James manoeuvred Lutwidge and two of his colleagues off the Board. A month later orders were given for work to extend the Old Pier by some thirty yards and to move the lighthouse a similar distance. Also a new Tongue, almost parallel to and about the same length as the Old (Merchants) Tongue, was built out from the end of Marlborough Street, 'in case it should be afterwards found necessary'. The Trustees also completed in 1743 extensive additions to the New Pier in order to accommodate vessels requiring deep water.

As a result of this dispute, Lowther's attitude to the Trustees had hardened. The concept of power-sharing was shelved indefinitely, with unfortunate long-term results for both town and Harbour.

Because of the prosperity of the Harbour, the improvements had been financed without the intervention of Sir James as shown by the Extract of Accounts for the six years ending 25 March 1746.

Disbursements:-

Debts repaid to Sir James per 1739 Act	938	17	8
Interest etc on above amount	62	12	8
Paid one Moiety of Cost of Act 13 Geo 2	95	7	3
Paid re Repairs of Harbour 1739/40	60	6	9
	£1157	4	4
Less Perpetual Duties Recd 1739/40	105	12	2
Debts Incurred before 1739 Act in force	1051	12	2
Cost of Deepening the Harbour in 1740	832	12	9
Cost of the New Pier 1742/45	5208	9	6
Ordinary Repairs to the Harbour 1740/46	1176	6	2
Interest on Money Borrowed	426	10	8
Cost of the Battery, Guns, Arms, Powder etc.	1121	18	9
Costs occasioned by the Rebellion 1745/46	478	18	5
	£10296	8	5

Incomes:-

Duties for Six Years	5584	4	4
Bonds—Borrowed and Outstanding	3895	0	0
Fines Received		13	4
Balance due to Treasurer, at 25 March 1746	816	10	9
	£10296	8	5

Of the Bonds Outstanding Sir James Lowther Held £1600.

These accounts are of particular interest as they show the greatly increased income from the duties, and also the significant sums paid out for the building of the forts as well as for the defence of the town at the time of the Second Jacobite Rebellion. Throughout the 1750s, the prosperity of the Harbour was such that these works were paid for without difficulty and, by 1760, the outstanding bonds had been reduced to £2,970, and the treasurer had a substantial balance in hand.

The Act of 1761

A minute of 29 November 1760 reads 'the Bounds of the Harbour for discharging Goods is now too little, and the Harbour should be extended to the East Side of the Sugar House Bulwark (previously the Counter Mole opposite Duke Street) and from there in a line therewith to Low-water Mark'.

The powers to levy the temporary duties expired on 21 April 1761, and because of the amount of work requiring to be done, it was felt necessary to petition for another Act of Parliament (1 Geo 3 Cap 44) in order to extend the duties for a further term.

A few important local families were regularly represented on the Board of Trustees. These were the overseas merchants, trading with the West Indies and the American colonies for sugar, rum, tobacco, timber, and slaves. Many of them established long-lasting connections with the New World, while others emigrated there. In the early part of the 18th century, six members of the Gale family served as Trustees, while a little later six members of the Gilpin family also served. Other well known families, including the Lutwidges and Littledales, were also represented. Among the major tobacco merchants were Peter How and John Younger, the employer of the young John Paul (Jones).

The nominees of Sir James Lowther were of a rather different background. His Whitehaven agents, first the Gilpins and later the Speddings, were always members of the Board, and a Spedding was invariably nominated as Sir James's deputy. The legal and financial people were also usually nominated by Lowther.

Sir James Lowther died in 1755, and the Whitehaven estate passed to Sir William Lowther of Marske and Holker. Sir William attended only one meeting of the Trustees and died the following year. The estate was then inherited by Sir James Lowther of Maulds Meaburn ('Wicked Jimmy'), who was created 1st Earl of Lonsdale in 1784.

John Spedding died in 1758 and in his role as Lowther's principal agent was followed by his nephew James. James, who was the son of Carlisle Spedding, also became treasurer and collector of duties for the Harbour.

Chapter 2

Harbour Improvements in the Later 18th Century

The Act of 1762

The population of Whitehaven increased from 2,222 in 1693 to 9,063 in 1762, and as a result was suffering from many problems. There were recurring difficulties involving the distribution of food and, because of the lack of a system of law enforcement, there was a great deal of crime and civil disturbance. The water supply was totally inadequate and, as there was no system of sewage disposal, the town was in a filthy condition, with consequent high levels of sickness and disease.

In 1756, Sir James Lowther of Maulds Meaburn was only 20 years of age, but he approached the affairs of his new estate with enthusiasm. After many meetings at Whitehaven, at which these matters were debated at great length, Sir James steered through Parliament the Act of 1762 (2 Geo 3 Cap 87) which contained many provisions for the town's government, in addition to some relating to the Harbour. The Act is important in the history of Whitehaven as it shows Sir James's intention to introduce measures for the better management of the town than was possible through his Manorial Court Leet. It also effectively gave the Board of Trustees some of the powers that they had long sought.

Under the new Act, the Board of Trustees was dismissed, and a new one formed. In fact, all the old members were re-appointed and all were required to serve until the first Friday in August 1769, when the tri-annual election of 14 of the Trustees was to recommence. Interestingly, only 13 elective Trustees were named in the Act, although a 14th was co-opted later. Previously, harbour works, once having been decided upon, could be started by any 11 Trustees, but under the new Act no works could be commenced without the approval of Lowther and 17 Trustees.

The temporary duties had been renewed until 10 April 1782 by the Act of 1761, but several items were now added to the list of items on which duties were payable. These were:

Every Ton of Rice	Two Shillings
Every 100 Deerskins	One Shilling
Every Ton of Logwood	One Shilling
Every Ton of Battery	Two Shillings

9 Watercolour by an unknown artist, 1780. In the foreground, riggers are fitting out a new vessel. Old Quay, with its lookout, projects from the left of the picture, whilst beyond the busy harbour, the Cumbrian coast is visible looking towards Parton and Workington. Reproduced by kind permission of Tullie House Museum, Carlisle.

In addition, after the expiry of the term, the permanent duties were to be increased to the whole of the rates on the tonnage of ships and to one third of the duty on coals and all other goods and merchandise.

With regard to town improvement matters, the two most important dealt with the provision of a water supply and also of street lighting. Powers were taken 'to convey water from certain springs arising in or near Stanley Wood ... by the nearest and most convenient Ways to and through the said Town of Whitehaven, and through every Street, Lane and Alley thereof and to the said Harbour thereof'.

'For Enlightening [sic] the Town of Whitehaven', the Trustees were enabled to 'set up Glass Lamps to be lit from Sunset to Sunrise from 20 August to 20 April yearly for ever'.

Although both schemes were approved by a majority of citizens at meetings held in the town, no action was taken to implement either for many years. After examining a scheme in which water was to be conveyed in pipes of bored out oak trees, the plan to supply water was abandoned. Apart from a supply provided privately by Lord Lonsdale in 1835, Whitehaven did not receive an adequate supply of water until 1850. Similarly, there was a long delay over the provision of street lighting, but some 150 oil lamps were eventually put up in 1781.

It seems most probable that the reason for these delays was one of finance. Although the Trustees were able to levy rates on property to cover the costs, they occasionally experienced difficulty in borrowing money by mortgaging Harbour duties for harbour works, and possibly felt that the mortgaging of rates would be even more difficult. Of course, there was also a great deal of resistance from potential ratepayers over the level of rates necessary.

The Harbour required the use of a large number of horses and carts, and 'whereas by the Negligence and Misbehaviour of Carters, Draymen and Waggoners', bye-laws were to be made for their better control. The River Pow and Bransty Beck, at this time open water-courses, were 'to be widened, covered and turned for preventing Nuisances and Obstructions being thrown therein'.

At the time of the passing of the 1762 Act, the Trustees had in mind two major extensions to the Harbour. The new Act described 'the extent of the Harbour to be enlarged': the boundaries were to be as laid down in the Act of 1708 with an addition to the north east towards Bransty, and thence to low-water mark. The first scheme was the lengthening of the New Pier by 40 yards, while the other was the building of a new mole—the North East Wall—angled at its extremity towards the new pier. This would have provided a well enclosed harbour of considerable extent, and powers were also granted to erect wet and dry docks and dockyards.

However, there was a body of opinion which thought these schemes too ambitious, and wished instead to extend the Old Pier and the Sugar Bulwark, thus creating a smaller harbour, but still well enclosed. In the event, the larger scheme was decided upon.

After much debate and consequent delay, work began on the extension to the New Pier in 1764, and was carried on simultaneously with the covering in of Pow Beck. Both works were undertaken by the same masons, who moved from one job to the other depending on the tide. The New Pier extension was not completed until 1767 due to a shortage of masons and because of difficulties in obtaining the requisite quantity of stones.

In the meantime, the Trustees were unable to decide exactly where to site the North East Wall, but eventually agreed that it should commence '160 yards North East of the Sugar House Bulwark, out to sea 216 yards, and from thence in a straight line West half South 95 yards ...'.

The confusion of the Trustees at this point is quite clear, as they also decided to lengthen the Old Pier, and to alter the Sugar House Bulwark, thus apparently beginning the smaller scheme, at the same time as work was being carried out on the larger one. Sir James Lowther insisted that the opinion of John Smeaton, civil engineer, be sought. Smeaton visited Whitehaven, and his advice dated 8 April 1768, was to lengthen the Old Pier by 30 yards, after which he would review the situation! Less than three weeks later, on 28 April 1768, orders were given to begin work on the new North East Mole and, it should be noted, at least with the acquiescence of Sir James Lowther.

The indecisiveness of the Trustees was not surprising perhaps, in view of the fluctuations in the volumes of trade through the Harbour. The war with France 1757/63, caused interruptions in trade with Europe and, at the same time, the tobacco trade from Virginia began a rapid decline. Whitehaven Harbour was still extremely busy, but the nature of the trade was changing. These factors obviously presented the Trustees with something of a dilemma, in that they were unable to assess the future require-ments of the Harbour with any degree of confidence. In fact, Whitehaven became increasingly dependent on exports of coal; by 1770, of the 200 ships belonging to the port, only 30 were not employed in the coal trade.

Work continued on the straight section of the North East Wall in desultory fashion. It was reported as being almost complete in 1775 when work had begun on the angled leg. Great difficulty was experienced in obtaining stone for the new mole and in 1780 the Sugar House Bulwark was shortened and the stones re-used in the new work. Much to Sir James's annoyance, the Trustees, in the following year, contracted with Lord Egremont for the extraction of stone from a quarry at Bransty, as the stone there was of better quality than that from Sir James's New Church quarry, which the Trus-tees were supposed to use. Some revision of the original plans for the wall was made in 1784, and it was eventually finished in 1790 after much pressure from Sir James, then Lord Lonsdale.

It will be noticed that the Trustees proceeded with their larger scheme during this period. John Smeaton visited Whitehaven in 1775 and again in 1783, but it would appear that any advice from him was ignored or, at best, was left in abeyance.

However, after the passing of the Act of 1762, the Trustees had few problems regarding financial matters. Apart from a short period when money was difficult to borrow (£400 only being received when £4,000 was advertised for), the duties pro-vided an income more than sufficient to meet all requirements. Harbour Bonds were issued, as before, and were readily repaid when due. In addition, The Trustees were able to borrow from the banks newly opened in the town from the late 1780s onwards.

The Act of 1788
In 1788, a short Act of Parliament (28 Geo 3 Cap 61) was obtained merely to renew the preceding Acts, and to renew the duties for a further term of 21 years.

In 1789, the Trustees came to the conclusion that the Harbour needed to be altered drastically. After polling local opinion, they advocated a scheme which envisaged

10 Watercolour by T. Askew, 1789. The North Wall extends across the picture, with Old Quay and what is now called Old New Quay, beyond. The huge structure centre left was the coal staithes. An engraving, possibly based on this painting was published in Hutchinson's *History of Cumberland* in 1794, but some of the detail is lacking. Reproduced by kind permission of Cumbria County Library Service, Carlisle.

demolishing 64 yards of the (new) North East Wall, adding 70 yards to the Old Pier and 75 yards to the Sugar House Bulwark. This, it was said, would provide space for 100 extra vessels in the Harbour. Concurrently, the Trustees reported that the Old Pier was in a 'dangerous and ruinous condition' and that the necessary repairs would cost £1,125. Before doing anything, therefore, they asked Lord Lonsdale for his views, but unfortunately his lordship did not always respond. It will be remembered that under the Act of 1762 the approval of Lord Lonsdale and of 17 Trustees was necessary before any works in the Harbour could be commenced.

Two years later, in January 1791, when the Old Pier was 'in imminent danger of collapse', two Trustees were despatched to press Lord Lonsdale for his opinions. His lordship replied in writing, and insisted that his letter be entered in the Minute Book verbatim 'that there be no mistake'. He wrote:

Ever since Lord Lonsdale has been in possession of the Whitehaven Estate, the Harbour of Whitehaven has been an object of his attention. And he has to lament that his sentiments for the Improvement of it have not received the approbation which he thinks they deserved: different opinions being adopted have proved fatal to the Harbour, Town and Shipping.

Lord Lonsdale gave his sentiments relative to an Erection for a North East Wall. Different Plans were laid on the Coffee House Table for many years, for the opinion of the Merchants, Masters of Ships and others (who might be supposed to know what ought to be done best for the Improvement of the Harbour) as well as before several different Setts of Trustees for their approbation. The Plan upon which the North East Wall is now built, was approved of as being most eligible. Lord Lonsdale was induced to acquiesce, as such was the opinion of the Trustees and Town tho' his sentiments were very different; not choosing to withhold his Consent when so many of the Merchants and Naval opinions approved of that Plan. But he could not help thinking that his own Ideas would have been more beneficial to the Harbour, and Time has proved that his Ideas have been just and right, for the Harbour has been detrimented by the contrary opinions being adopted.

Lord Lonsdale has seen many Plans as propositions for the alterations of the Harbour of Whitehaven. Not one of them has been approved by the Trustees or the Town. It was his wish that an Engineer should be consulted. With a great deal of Trouble and Difficulty, he obtained the presence of Mr Smeaton (the first Engineer in the Kingdom) to view and inspect the Harbour and to lay his Propositions before the Trustees, with great Inconvenience to Lord Lonsdale being at that time very much occupied with business.

But Lord Lonsdale's Endeavours were again frustrated, and the Trustees, totally disapproving of what Mr Smeaton had plann'd, and the Trustees not agreeing upon a Plan of their own, the Harbour remains as it was ...

The Trustees, unperturbed, immediately came up with a scheme, including plans 'to Extend the Old Pier 50 yards, and to widen and lengthen the Bulwark ...'. This was nothing more than the 'smaller' scheme of the 1760s, but it was sent off to Lord Lonsdale, who again did not respond. And again nothing was done.

The Trustees found that Sir James was not the easiest man with whom to deal. For many years, meetings of Trustees seem to have been held only when Sir James was present. The several Acts of Parliament did not specify at what intervals Lowther was to exercise his right to nominate Trustees, and only very infrequently did he do so. In practice he seems to have preferred to attend the meetings himself along with his agent Spedding. Meetings, in fact, were held at irregular intervals, and in some years only the June accounts meeting took place. The tri-annual election of Trustees was held as required by the Acts, but it is noticeable that attendance was poor, as many meetings were adjourned through lack of a quorum.

From 1770 onwards, Sir James attended fewer meetings, though the number of meetings increased quite dramatically. In 1775, for instance, 10 were held, and in 1778, no fewer than nineteen. The relationship between his lordship and the Trustees continued to be an uneasy one, and the Earl's attitude is perhaps best illustrated by a minute which appears immediately before one of the tri-annual elections of Trustees.

> 2 July 1793—The Trustees request Mr Garforth to acquaint His Lordship that a General Election of Trustees would be held on 2 August next, and they wish to know before the time the alterations he pleases to make.

However, the Trustees carried on with the day to day business of the Harbour as is shown by the following minutes:

> 2 November 1767—Widow Rawling, Scavenger, to be paid £16 from 1 July 1765 to date and discharged for not keeping clean the keys [sic] and wharfs.

> 28 October 1774—Peter How, Trustee, is now dead. William Hicks is appointed in his room. James Grayson, Assistant Pier Master, is now dead. John Robinson is appointed in his room.

Although after 1760 the tobacco trade had declined rapidly, and during the 1790s coal exports were much reduced, the Harbour was still busy and overcrowded. From the minutes of the Trustees, it appears that the Board was expecting the initiative regarding Harbour developments to come from Lord Lonsdale, even though they tended to ignore his recommendations regarding schemes of which they did not approve. On the other hand, the Trustees had ideas of their own which they were loath to implement without Lonsdale's approval and, since his lordship often chose to ignore the Trustees, little was done.

In matters of town government, Lord Lonsdale was no more willing than his predecessors to concede any form of power sharing. Unfortunately, following the retirement of James Spedding in 1788, the efficiency of his representation in Whitehaven declined rapidly and, as Lonsdale was largely preoccupied elsewhere, it is clear that matters were simply drifting along, to the detriment of both the town and the Harbour.

The Act of 1792

The North East Wall proved to be unsatisfactory, and yet another scheme was proposed in which was envisaged the building of a wall nearer to Redness Point. This required an extension of the Harbour, and a further Act of Parliament was required to formalise the boundaries of the additional area. This was done in 1792 by 32 Geo 3 Cap 75.

This Act contained an interesting provision regarding the legal status of the Board of Trustees. Prior to this date, because the Board was not a body corporate, any legal action was abated on a change of Trustees. A clerk was now appointed, and actions both by and against the Board were to be taken in his name, and could not be abated if he were replaced, or even on his death.

During the 1790s, matters were at a low ebb at Whitehaven. Following the American War of Independence (1776-83), during which many of the ships belonging to the port were lost and the tobacco trade finally ceased, England was again at war with France, this time as a result of the French Revolution. During these periods trading patterns were severely interrupted and Whitehaven became even more dependent on the coal trade. Unfortunately, owing to the incompetence of Lonsdale's agent, Thomas Wylie, even this was in decline, reaching only 60 per cent of the levels attained in the 1760s. The Harbour was in decay, piers were crumbling, and the coal-handling facilities were not being maintained.

Yet, in spite of the muddle regarding the development and alteration of the piers and wharfs, the Harbour continued to be busy and prosperous. One example of the Harbour accounts taken from this period indicates the level of activity and also the range of services, which included street cleaning and street lighting, provided.

Year Ended 25 March 1794			
Extract from the Treasurer's Accounts			
Balance in Hand at 25 March 1793	227	1	5
Received from Collector	1668	0	0
	1895	1	5
Disbursements:-			
Cost of Harbour Works and Repairs	1046	10	11
Cost of Operating Hoppers	241	6	6
Gunpowder and Various—Voluntary Fund	105	9	8
Cost of Scavenger	98	0	4
Cost of Lighting Town and Harbour	170	1	10
	1661	9	3
Balance in Hand at 25 March 1794	233	12	2
Extract from the Collector's Accounts.			
Harbour Duties Received	1848	4	8
Lighting Rate—Harbour	136	16	11
Lamp and Scavenger Rate—Town	210	0	0
	2195	1	7
Paid to Treasurer	1668	0	0
Balance paid to Moore, Hamilton & Co Bank	£527	1	7

The balance at the bank at this date was £3,908 6s. 8d., only two years after the repayment of bonds totalling £5,100.

The lighting rate collected from ships using the Harbour represents, at 1d. per ton, 32,843 tons. Assuming the average tonnage of the vessels to be 125 tons, approximately 270 ships paid tonnage duty during the year. This rate, of course was levied only once each year.

Before the end of the 18th century, the Board of Trustees had changed considerably in character. The transatlantic merchants had virtually disappeared, and their places had been taken by lawyers, doctors, bankers, clergymen and important tradesmen of

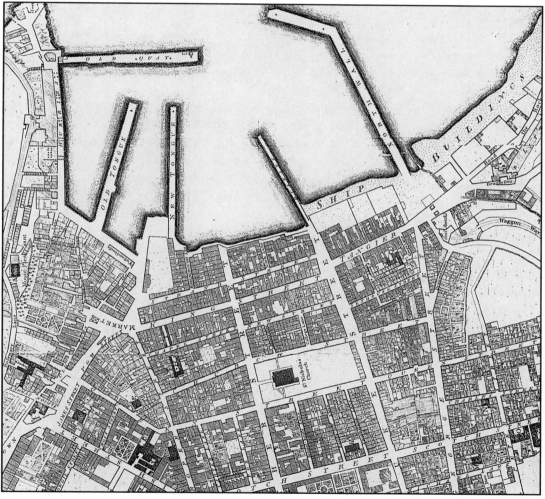

11 This map is taken from *A Plan of the Town and Harbour of Whitehaven in the County of Cumberland*, from an actual survey, Anno. 1790 by J. Howard.

the town. The Jeffersons, trading with the West Indies, were almost the last of the overseas merchants. They joined the Board during the 1790s, along with Knubley and Garforth who were lawyers, Dixon, a doctor, Hamilton and Sargeant, bankers, the Revs. Huddleston and Milner, clergymen, and Hartley, Benn, and Hogarth, manufacturers and tradesmen. These men were all well known in the town, and in their time had a significant impact on the economic and social life of Whitehaven.

The task of the Trustees was never an easy one throughout the 18th century, particularly with regard to matters affecting town government. Despite the many Acts of Parliament, the real powers of the Trustees had not been properly defined, nor had the relative roles of Lonsdale, the Trustees and the Court Leet. The real power, of course, remained with the Lord of the Manor, Lonsdale, and it was not until 1859 that an attempt was made to improve the situation.

Although it was not recognised at the time, Whitehaven had passed its peak as a port with a significant overseas trade. Shipments of coal, however, continued to increase and, with the later addition of large tonnages of iron ore, it continued to be a busy place.

The Harbour of Whitehaven was, like the town, basically a creation of the 18th century. It was built, rebuilt and altered several times in order to try to meet the requirements of those using it. In spite of financial problems in the first half of the century, and in spite of difficulties in deciding how best the Harbour should be developed, the Trustees had done their best to meet those requirements. Certain major developments needed to be undertaken during the 1790s, but the opportunity was missed, and it was left to the early years of the next century before further improvements were made.

Chapter 3

Day by Day Operations—18th Century

Repairs and Maintenance

Once the Trustees had taken control of the Harbour in 1709, they were confronted with many operational problems. Experience soon showed that chief among these was that the piers and quays were in constant need of repair. Most structural damage was done by the weather, but some was done by the ships using the Harbour, and some was caused by inherent weaknesses in the original building design.

The west coast of Cumberland is subject, of course, to frequent storms, like the one in 1720 which seriously damaged the Old Pier. The Trustees ordered that 'the Pier head be immediately secured as well as possible with Timber and Plank, and that the Holes in the Stone Work be filled up and spiled, and that such other care as is necessary be taken'. The Trustees' minutes record a great many such incidents, but none so damaging as the great storm of January 1796. The minute for 25 January reads:

> In consequence of Damage the Harbour this day sustained, viz, The New Quay being broke up by the Violence of the Sea from the Fort to the North West Corner being a space of about 80 yards nearly to the foundation of the same. The New Tongue and Bulwark much shaken and damaged. The Quay extending from Tom Herd Rock to the Half Moon Battery totally destroyed and the Half Moon Battery nearly in the same situation, also Old and New Forts very much damaged. The House lately purchased by the Trustees in danger of coming down.

The Trustees ordered that the Harbour be made as secure as possible, and wrote off to Sir James Lowther for advice.

Occasionally, damage was caused by ships being driven on to the piers by stormy weather. At a meeting called specially on 16 September 1783 to consider 'Storm Damage to the Old Key', it is noted that 'A Ship drove upon and very much injured, the interior angle of the Old Key, and as the Season is now so far advanced, that it is not prudent to take down the said angle and undertake a thorough repair'. All was made as secure as possible, and more complete repairs were undertaken at a later date.

High tides and consequent flooding were also a problem. In 1724, 'The Breach in the Counter Mole and the damage done to the Beck Wall by the late great Floods ...' were ordered to be repaired immediately.

In their early years, the Trustees were subject to severe financial constraints, and no doubt the new quays were built with as little expenditure as possible. In any case, huge amounts of timber were used in construction, and even the use of mortar is doubtful. The start of the first mole from the bottom of Lowther Street in 1709 was delayed for several months for want of '30 Tons of Squared Oak'. It was eventually obtained from Ireland. The specifications for all the structures built in the early part of the century always required 'Framing'. For instance the head of the Counter Mole from Duke Street was 'to be framed with Timber in a suitable manner'. Again, in 1718, when the mole was being altered, 'That an Addition of some few courses of Stones be made at the End of the Counter Mole well Framed, the Frame Ends to be Bolted into the Present Frames'.

Ships' masters must have found the frames ideally suitable for mooring their ships, but it was made an offence to do so: 'Ships Masters are guilty of damaging Framework and Fenders belonging to the Harbour, by fastening their Ends to them in Hauling etc.- To desist at once, Penalty 20/-'.

It seems possible that the original quays were built of timber, and the stones laid without mortar. As repairs became necessary, the timber was removed and the stones properly laid. For instance in 1732, 'the Head of the Countermole to be repaired, and the Upper Course of Stones laid in Lime'. During the 1730s repairs to the Harbour cost, on average, a little over £150 per annum. Ten years later this had risen to almost £200.

Pow Beck and the Inner Harbour

Judging by the number of references to it in the minutes of the Trustees, Pow Beck must have been a constant source of trouble during the first half of the 18th century.

In 1709 Pow Beck was an open stream, running through James Street, Pow Street and the market place, and entering the Harbour in front of the Custom House. Most of the people of Whitehaven lived very close to the beck, and they used it as a depository for all their ordure, rubbish, ashes and so on. In short, Pow Beck was an open sewer. The filth was washed into the Harbour, where it was taken out to sea, but brought back in again by the following tide. Over the years, many costly attempts were made to deal with this accumulation of filth, but with little success. The appointment of a scavenger under the Act of 1708 was effectively obstructed by the attitude of the Court Leet.

It is recorded on 20 September 1709, that it was proposed 'To employ men and carts to remove Gravel, Clay and Tangle for the purpose of Cleaning, Deepening, Levelling and Ordering the Current and Course of the Pow Beck'. Similar work was again carried out in December of the same year 'to equalize the flow to the Harbour'.

In August 1719, the Trustees turned down what must have been an interesting proposition to cover in Pow Beck 'and to build houses thereon'. It was noted that the course of the beck was again a cause for concern.

A few years later it was decided to employ three or four men whose job it would be to keep the beck clean and flowing. They were to be responsible to the Harbour Master. Sir James had given instructions that the Court Leet was to be responsible for keeping the streets clean, but the Trustees took the view that the beck was properly a Harbour matter.

After the building of the Old or Merchants Quay, it was found that sand was collecting between the end of the quay and the end of the Old Pier. To correct this problem, it was decided that boards should be spiked to the bed of the Harbour to alter the course of the beck, and to wash away the accumulated sand. This was not the end of this particular difficulty, but the Trustees found they were presented with an even more difficult version of it after the New Tongue was built.

In 1751, it was acknowledged that the beck was not keeping the inner Harbour clean, nor was it removing accumulations of sand. Again, a person was to be employed 'to prevent people from throwing rubbish into the Beck, thus blocking the flow needed to sluice the Harbour'.

Finally, the Act of 1761 gave powers 'to deepen and cover Pow Beck because of Dirt, Sullage, and the Wash of the Streets falling into the Beck and filling up the Harbour'. The work was quickly completed, and although the citizens then went to the Harbour side to dispose of their garbage, the problem was greatly alleviated, because the Harbour was found to be easier to clean than the beck.

The overseas merchants were continually pressing for a deep water harbour to the seaward side of the Old Pier, but Sir James and the Trustees were not prepared to agree to this plan and, instead, many attempts were made to deepen the inner Harbour. For instance, in 1739 it was resolved 'to deepen the Inner Harbour along the inside of the Merchants Quay, and other parts of the Harbour, for the convenience of unloading Foreign Goods and Merchandize and to make more room

12　The Pow Beck culvert under repair in 1927.

for coal ships to lie when detained by Contrary Winds, Embargos and want of Convoy in time of War'.

After the building of the New Pier in the 1750s, work was carried out on deepening the inside of it 'to make room for as many ships to lye there as can conveniently'. In 1777, the Trustees were informed that, because of the constant deepening, the bed of the inner Harbour was 10 feet lower than the foundations of the adjacent Wharf walls. Some walls had to be demolished and rebuilt on deeper foundations.

Ballast

In order to control the movement of ballast in the Harbour, the 1762 Act authorised the purchase of four hoppers from Messrs. Richard Liddell and Henry Bird at North Shields, 'to carry Ballast out to sea to such a distance as to prevent its return by the flux of the sea'.

Over many years the Trustees tried to provide a deep, clean harbour with a smooth and level bottom. In the last respect, they were constantly hindered by ships' masters who insisted on discharging their ballast over the side of their vessels into the Harbour.

In order to stop this nuisance, the following rules were imposed:

1) No ballast to be unloaded into the Harbour during the night - Penalty for each offence £10.
2) Masters not to use carts or coups except in necessity, and then each cart or coup to be 4' 6" long and 15" deep. - Penalty 20/- per load.
3) Masters requiring Ballast not to take from other ships, except with leave in writing signed by seven Trustees, but from the Harbour as directed by the pier master - Penalty for each offence 20/-.
4) Ballast not to be put on keys - Penalty £3.

A buoy was fixed outside the Harbour and masters were instructed that ballast was only to be discharged outside the limit set by it.

The Trustees had the greatest difficulty in enforcing these regulations, and several ships' masters were disciplined for their offences: 'James McQuillon, Master of the Brig James was fined £10 for dumping Ballast into a Hopper during the night. On appeal, the fine was mitigated to 20/-'. In another case 'John Graham, Master of the Sloop, Vulture, was fined £100 for discharging his Ballast into his own Boat thereby defrauding the Hoppers. But in consideration of some extenuating circumstances the fine was mitigated to 20/-'. Unfortunately, in neither case is any indication given of what the mitigating circumstances were which merited such a large reduction of the original fines!

The Hoppers

During the 1750s, the Trustees had on hire two hoppers, a type of sailing barge, for carrying ballast and sullage out to sea. These were extremely successful, and it was decided to keep the two already in use and to order two more. The hoppers were still in service in 1793, when it was decided to purchase an additional vessel of about 70 tons burthen 'as the present ones are insufficient for the service'.

Hulks and Old Ships

Some of the ships' masters and owners were guilty of the most annoying practice of leaving their ships moored to a quay for long periods of time. This was yet another problem which the Trustees seemed unable to solve. It was a cause for complaint throughout the century, in spite of the threat of a penalty of 10s. for each day the ship remained in position after the expiry of four months.

The worst case reported concerned the brig John which, in 1775, had been lying between the Old and New Tongues for upwards of two years. During the whole of the period no work had been carried out on the vessel and, indeed, it appeared to have been abandoned. All the Trustees could do was to order the pier master to move it outside the New Tongue.

Usually, such ships were left in the inner Harbour between Merchants Quay and West Wharf, and the pier master was instructed to move them to the outside of Merchants Quay, near to the Sugar Bulwark. This then released space much needed for other vessels. It was decreed that ships would not be allowed to lie thus moored for longer than four months.

The Fire Engines

The wooden ships in use at the time were a serious fire hazard, and although restrictive Harbour regulations were in force, nevertheless accidental fires were not an uncommon occurrence. There were no fire fighting facilities available at Whitehaven until 1727, when 'as a matter of great urgency' it was decided to obtain 'a water engine for extinguishing fires, of such size as Mr Lowther shall judge convenient'. This machine was shipped from London, but it may not have been suitable, as in 1739 it was considered that 'the procuring of a couple of Engines for the Quenching of Fire' ought to be actioned without delay. One fire engine, complete with 40 feet of pipe, and brass screws, was bought from Mr. Newsham of London at a cost of £70 7s. 6d. When it arrived at Whitehaven, it was kept in Holy Trinity church. It can only be supposed that, at some specific fire, the equipment was found wanting, for some years later, in 1748, the treasurer was instructed to procure from Dublin '50 Leathern Buckets for use with the Fire Engines' as a matter of great urgency.

Apparently, the fire engines were still not satisfactory, for five years later what would appear to be a replacement machine was purchased. This time a man, George Ritson, was found to repair and look after the machines, and he received a salary of £4 a year: 'The said Engines with Leathern Buckets and Pipes belonging to the same be removed from Trinity Chapel to the little Store Room for that purpose lately erected on the ground within the limits of the Harbour in the West Strand.' There were three keys for the shed Ritson had one, the pier master had one, and the other was kept in the Watch House.

Following a fire in 1785, when the fire engines did not perform adequately, the treasurer and pier master were ordered 'to inspect the state of the Fire Engines, and put them forthwith into the most complete repair, and provide whatever may be wanted to them for the safety of the public'. The repaired engines were to be 'taken out and worked once a quarter'. Several of the Harbour boatmen received ex gratia payments from the voluntary fund for their 'exertions at the late fire'.

Sundry Items
Accidents to Ships
In June 1792, in bad weather, an accident was caused by the alleged negligence of the Harbour boatmen, employees of the Harbour Trust. A ship from Barnstaple was driven onto the Old Pier and dashed to pieces because the Harbour boatmen ignored signals from the vessel indicating that it wished to moor. The lives of the crew were saved with difficulty, as they had to be dragged with ropes over the battlement onto the Pier. The Master of the Harbour Boats claimed that he was busy attending other ships, but as a result of the incident he was reduced to the rank of common boatman. Three other men were rewarded with one guinea each for their work in the rescue.

The Firing of Weapons
Britain was often at war during the 18th century, and during those periods merchant ships usually carried guns, and the crews were armed with hand guns and cutlasses. When in port, members of the crew were given to discharging their firearms at the least excuse.

Whitehaven Harbour had a rule prohibiting this practice, first introduced in August 1743. It reads: 'As a result of someone having lost his life, the firing of Guns, Muskets, and Pistols from on Board any Ship or Vessel in the Harbour, is prohibited'. This order was renewed in 1746 and again in 1763, when a penalty of £1 for each offence was introduced. This rule must have been extremely difficult to enforce, particularly as people on board ships were encouraged to fire off their weapons during an event of celebration, such as a Lonsdale visit to Whitehaven.

The Treatment of Workpeople
There are several recorded cases of men being injured or falling ill in the course of working at the Harbour. Although the men were not always employed by the Trust, usually the Trustees paid doctors' bills, and/or made ex gratia payments to the sufferer or his immediate family.

Mr. Hamilton was paid £5 3s. 4d. 'for dressing the men wounded in the Harbour Works for the three years 1742, 3 and 4'. At a later date the Trustees agreed to pay the surgeon's bill in respect of 'Samuel Roper, an old Labourer for cure of a wound received in the Quarries last Winter - £2.18. 6.'. The quarries referred to were at Bransty and leased by the Trustees. Poor Samuel Roper was involved in another accident five years later when he was 'lamed at work', and had to have his arm amputated. The Trustees paid Dr. Harris £4 18s. 8d. for performing the operation.

Occasionally, the Trustees made payments to parties injured in the strangest circumstances: 'A Hopper in a Gale, crushed the fishing boat of John Dixon, a poor fisherman. He, his wife and seven children have been reduced to the greatest necessity'. Dixon was awarded 10s. 6d. in recompense. This award was made as a result of an appeal for help by Mrs. Dixon. A second remarkable incident involved David Casson, a waterman. He was taking water to a ship at the hurries when his skull was fractured by a flying piece of stone, following an explosion when blasting on the rocks. Casson received £4 from the Voluntary Fund.

In 1794 the Trustees received bills totalling £42, from the executors 'of those Seamen who suffered in the West Indies from Yellow Fever'. These were paid from the Voluntary Fund, apparently as a charitable donation.

Staff

The Pier Master

To carry out all the duties and enforce the many regulations, the Trustees employed only three staff. The Act of 1708 provided for a pier master, a collector of duties and a secretary/treasurer, and this was the staffing level maintained until 1763, when it was agreed that the work of the pier master had become too much for one man. Later in the century, assistants were also found for the treasurer, in order to collect rates and other amounts due to the Trustees.

The first employee appointed by the Trustees in 1709 was Peter Senhouse as pier master at a salary of £20 per annum. His first task was to write 'Rules regarding the Mooring and Berthing of Ships, the Unloading and Scattering of Ballast, the positioning of Mooring Posts, and the keeping tidy of the Pier and Wharf'. These were rules which he was then required to enforce. Senhouse was dismissed in 1722 because 'he has not done his duty as he ought to have done'. It was found that at the time of his dismissal he owed £15 7s. 9d. to the Harbour. Incredibly, it was agreed that Senhouse would not have to repay this amount, 'in Consideration of his extraordinary services'!

In 1726 the pier master was required to keep a light at the pier head from 1 August to 1 May so long as there was a depth of water there of nine feet. The Trustees were to pay for the lanthorn, candles and oil, and were also to pay the pier master an additional £6 per year. When this particular pier master died, the Trustees agreed that his widow could continue to position the light on the pier, for the same fee, for the rest of her life.

One incumbent pier master, John Fox, had the misfortune to break both his legs in an accident while at work. The Trustees immediately gave him £20, a full year's salary, and continued to make regular payments to him for some years afterwards.

In 1760, the salary of the pier master was increased to £30, and it was agreed that an assistant was necessary. He was made responsible for a 'District', which extended to the two tongues and two tiers of ships on the west side of the Old Tongue. For this he received £20 per annum and in addition £10 for the care and management of the four hoppers.

Perhaps surprisingly, it was not until 1764 that any sort of accommodation at the Harbour was provided for the pier master. In that year a house was erected near the lighthouse on Old Pier for the hawsers, capstan bars and other materials. The building included a room 'for the resort of the Pier Master and Harbour Boatmen to attend the Tides and assist Ships as required'. The pier master was given an extra 30s. a year 'to furnish this room sufficiently with Firing'.

Not all ships' masters readily accepted the instructions of, or interpretation of the rules by, the pier master, and occasionally cases were taken before the Trustees for adjudication. For example, on 7 November 1786:

> Simon Fisher, Master of the Brigantine Mary (144 tons), did violently and insolently refuse and neglect to obey and comply with the orders and regulations, which to him the Pier Master, in the Execution of his Office seemed meet and reasonable in regard to the mooring, anchoring, laying and heaving of the vessel.

Fisher was fined five guineas and the Trustees 'required that the said Simon Fisher do under his hand acknowledge the outrage and offence he has committed against the Office of the Pier Master, and declare his sorrow for his behaviour, and that the said acknowledgement, and copies thereof be posted up in those parts of the Harbour appointed by the Act'. There were several such incidents over many years, but no other was quite so grandly reported.

The Collector of Duties

To fill the post of collector of duties, the Trustees in 1709 appointed Richard Gibson. He was paid 12d. in the pound of the duties and payments collected by him, but had to provide a surety of £500. All the monies received were paid over to the treasurer.

At his first meeting with the Trustees, Gibson produced a list of 47 ships which he had measured in accordance with the Act, and on which he had charged tonnage duty. The smallest was the *John of Dumfries*, at 13 tons, and the largest the *Friendship of Whitehaven*, 190 tons.

On 5 May 1740 it was resolved that 'Mr Gibson, being by Infirmities rendered incapable of personally executing the Office of Collector of Harbour Duties be discharged'. Lowther Spedding was appointed in his place. Whether Mr. Gibson received any form of recognition for his 30 years' service is not mentioned.

Lowther Spedding held this position until his death in 1746. His father, John, then combined the job with that of secretary/treasurer until 1758, when John's nephew James Spedding succeeded him. In the last decade of the century, following the death of the then incumbent, the position of collector was done away with, and the various duties were collected by an officer of the customs nominated by Lord Lonsdale.

The Rate Collector

The Act of 1739 provided for the reappointment of a scavenger, and the powers to levy a rate on property in order to defray the costs involved. A rate collector was found necessary to formulate a rate book and to ensure that property owners and occupiers paid the amounts due. The man appointed was Richard Oyes, who received a salary of 40s. a year, and was responsible to the treasurer. Following the introduction of street lighting in 1781, the salary of Oyes was increased to 80s. per annum plus an additional 40s. for collecting the lamp rate. After 42 years' service, Oyes was dismissed by the Trustees, but the dismissal was overruled by Lord Lonsdale, as his approval had not been sought. Oyes was reinstated, and he continued in service until 1793, a total of 50 years.

The Secretary/Treasurer

The first man appointed as secretary/treasurer was John Spedding, who held the position until his death in 1758. Throughout the whole period of his tenure of office his remuneration consisted only of nominal annual sums for registering the accounts. He had a series of successors, until in 1792 the legal position of the Board of Trustees was changed. Under that Act, a clerk was appointed, and actions by and against the Board, were taken in his name, and could not be abated even on his death.

The existing secretary/treasurer was dismissed, and Joseph Yeoward appointed as clerk at a salary of £60 a year. The financial arrangements were also changed. Although Yeoward was also treasurer, he was responsible only for disbursements made by the Trustees. Separate collectors for scavenger and lamp rate and for hopper dues were made responsible for their own accounts.

The Church Affair

On 28 February 1788, the Trustees 'Ordered that the Rev. Charles Cobbe Church be this day discharged from the Office of Treasurer, Receiver or Collector of the Harbour Dues, and all other Offices and Concerns of the Harbour of Whitehaven, and that William Wilson be appointed in his place'. Church had been appointed perpetual curate of Holy Trinity church in 1781, and had become treasurer to the Trustees in 1784.

At the time of his dismissal, there were many complaints from the creditors of the Trustees that they had not been paid amounts due to them although, it was disclosed, Church had some £6,400 of the Harbour fund in his keeping. Church would not reveal the whereabouts of this money when required to produce it, and also refused to pay it over to Wilson, the new treasurer. Further, he also refused to hand over his books, documents and accounts. The Trustees suspected that Church had invested the money for his own benefit, but were unable to obtain any information. They were placed in a position of some difficulty, as they were forced to borrow from their bank, Messrs. Moore Hamilton & Co, on overdraft.

In his position as treasurer, Church had been required to enter into sureties in case of his default and, at the time, bonds were held to a total value of £6,000. After taking Counsel's opinion, a writ was issued against Mr. Church, and the bonds were sent to London via Lord Lonsdale's solicitor. In August 1788, Church and his attorney tendered to the Trustees papers and money which purported to settle the account, but the Trustees declared that, as a bill had been filed in the Court of Chancery against Church, they were precluded from accepting the papers and money offered.

At the end of the year, Garforth, Lonsdale's solicitor, informed the Trustees that he had received £4,000 from Church, and that the money was to be sent by post to Whitehaven in packets of £500 in Bank of England notes. By June 1789, £3,000 had been transferred by this means, and paid into the bank account where it was urgently needed.

Despite attempts by the Trustees to collect the books and papers held by Church, and attempts by Church to deliver them, this matter was not resolved until 1805 following a final decision on the case given by the Solicitor General. At this time, the amount still owing to the Trustees was £3,800. Church had paid over this amount 10 years previously to his legal advisers who had invested it in three per cent Consolidated Bank annuities. The Solicitor General ruled that the annuities be sold and the proceeds transferred to the Trustees, who were to pay Church's costs from the accrued interest. Following 17 years of litigation, the cash was eventually received at Whitehaven on 5 April 1805. No further proceedings were taken in the matter, and Mr. Church continued as incumbent of Holy Trinity church until his death in 1808, when a plaque was placed in the church to commemorate his 27 years of service as minister. For over twenty years Church was also rector of Gosforth.

Chapter 4

Trade through Whitehaven Harbour

Exports

The Coal Trade

Sir Christopher Lowther, in 1633/4, built the first pier at Whitehaven principally to facilitate the export, not of coals, but of salt from saltpans which he owned. At the time, very little was known in the area about the techniques of mining coal, and consequently little was worked. During the 1630s some small tonnages were produced; for the saltpans, for local consumption, and some which was transported to Ireland and sold in Dublin. Only a small number of very small ships was available, but in 1636, for instance, some 2,400 tons of coal were exported.

When Sir Christopher died in 1644, his son and heir, John, was less than two years old. The Whitehaven estates lay fallow during Sir John's minority, but in 1655 he began in earnest to develop the coal industry there. The demand for coal in Dublin had increased substantially, and the pier, built by his father, was a great advantage in facilitating the loading of ships.

One of Sir John's first actions was to increase the length of the pier, the work being completed in 1665. As estate steward, he then appointed Thomas Tickell, a man who served diligently and efficiently from 1666 until 1692, and as mines manager, Thomas Jackson, who was experienced in the operation of coal mines. In order to expand coal production, Sir John began to seek out and buy coal-bearing land in the vicinity of Whitehaven, and within a few years had spent £11,000 on purchases. He also encouraged ships' masters to load coals for Ireland, and in the 1660s some 25 small ships were thus employed. Sir John tried to persuade ship owners to build bigger ships as he was disappointed to find that those in service carried only 30 to 40 tons on each voyage.

Tickell and Jackson were successful in boosting coal production, 90 per cent of which was exported to Ireland. However, there were problems. Although Sir John had succeeded in gaining a dominant position in the Irish market, he was aware of increasing competition from the coalfields in Scotland, Lancashire and Wales. In addition, coal owners at Workington and Ellenfoot (Maryport) were beginning to take an interest in the trade.

When they were loaded on to a ship, the coals were sold to the ship's master who on arrival at Dublin sold them through an agent for the highest possible price. However, the Lord Mayor of Dublin had powers to fix the price and as Dublin thus effectively controlled the on-board price at Whitehaven, Sir John was committed to ensuring that the costs of producing coal and taking it to the Harbour were kept as low as possible. He was discouraged by the high cost of mine development, which became necessary as the pits nearest to the Harbour became worked out. Coal was first worked from outcrops in the Howgill area, and operations were seriously impeded by the lack of the technology required to drain water from the mines. Thus it became necessary to open new pits further away from the Harbour, and as the distance from the mines to the Harbour increased, so did the cost of transport.

By the early 1680s, the Harbour was overcrowded and, as Sir John declined to take any action to improve the facilities, some of the coal merchants attempted to have improvements made to the nearby harbour at Parton. Writing some years later, John Spedding recorded that, in view of all the circumstances, Sir John considered leaving the coal trade, and actually went so far as to offer to lease the collieries for £300 per annum to John Gale, who by that time was colliery steward.

However, over a period of several years many of these problems were overcome. The driving of the Bannock Band Surface Water Level by Thomas Jackson, from the Ginns underneath Monkwray, made available an area of coals sufficient for many years. The introduction of corves into the mines facilitated the hoisting of coals to the surface, while the problem of finding a quicker and cheaper way of moving coals to the Harbour was solved by John Gale, who suggested using carts instead of pack horses. Because of the appalling state of the roads, the carts, drawn by horses, ran on parallel planks bounded on each side by baulks of timber. The 'Causey', as it was called, was built to link Woodagreen Pit with the Harbour in 1682/3 and was very successful. Sir John, unable to contemplate the export of coals from Parton, leased from the Crown all the land between high and low water marks there and, by taking out an injunction against the merchants, was able to forestall their projected pier.

As a result of these measures, trade continued to be profitable, and in 1687 Sir John again extended the length of the pier. However, several smaller coal owners, who were mining at Distington, Moresby, and Aikbank, again tried to promote the development of Parton in order to avoid payment of the fee charged by Lowther for the use of his pier. This time Sir John was put to a great deal of trouble in buying out or leasing their mines.

At about this time the Prior Band, the thickest and best seam of coal in the Whitehaven area, was discovered. In order to win it, pits were sunk in the Ginns area, and an abundant supply of high quality coal became available. By 1700, coal exports to Ireland had reached an annual average of 20,000 tons. This required (in 1702) the use of 79 ships, of which 39 were over 100 tons burthen, 30 were between 50 and 100 tons, and only 10 were below 50 tons. Each vessel, on average, completed perhaps five return voyages from Whitehaven to Dublin each year, and consequently there were some 350-400 departures each year of ships carrying coals from the Harbour.

The average of 25,000 tons of coal per annum was reached in 1705, when it was admitted that 'The Coal Trade at Whitehaven is now become the only support of the place and also of the adjoyning Country'. During the following years, output and exports of coal increased at a rapid rate, the average annual tonnage reaching 50,000 in 1717. Unfortunately, this was followed by a period of severe recession from which the trade did not recover until 1725, after which exports again increased rapidly. 75,000 tons per annum were sold by 1730, but in the later years of that decade, although demand was still increasing in Dublin, exports from Whitehaven became static at a little below 90,000 tons as competition from elsewhere took an increasing share of the trade. It was from this time that shipments from Workington became a significant proportion of the traffic to Ireland.

Although exports of coal through Whitehaven Harbour had more than trebled in 30 years, this had not been achieved without great difficulty. Adverse winds and bad weather often ensured that a large number of ships arrived simultaneously, thereby glutting the market with coals, which depressed the selling price. At times when prices in Dublin were low, some ships' masters opted to take cargoes from Ireland to Virginia or Norway, thus creating a shortage of ships. Attempts by John Spedding to increase the price on board ship at Whitehaven were often thwarted by the ships' masters who refused to take coals until the price was reduced.

Lowther, advised by John Spedding, tried to overcome these shipping problems by buying controlling shares in several vessels, in order that he could determine their movements. Profitability in the shipping trade was not high, however, and at times even Sir James diverted ships to Virginia in the hope of improving returns. Spedding's accounts demonstrated that capital was more profitably invested in mining operations than in ships, so consequently Lowther's shipping interests were only on a small scale.

Lowther and Spedding made many attempts to persuade the ships' masters to take coals to destinations in Ireland other than Dublin, setting the example by shipping cargoes to Cork and Limerick using Lowther-controlled ships. A scheme was tried in which the ships' masters were required to enter into a bond of £20 or £30 not to trade with Dublin, in return for which they were allowed to load out of turn on return to Whitehaven. These plans met with little success, as did attempts to persuade Irish ships' masters to collect coals at Whitehaven for discharge at ports other than Dublin.

Throughout the 18th century, Britain was frequently at war, most often with France. Collier ships trading with Ireland were often captured by the enemy, and were only recoverable on payment of a large ransom. As a result, the ships' masters refused to sail without a naval escort and, because one was only rarely available, coal movements were seriously interrupted. Attempts were made to arm vessels from private sources, and indeed, later in the century, Lowther provided escorts armed with guns borrowed from the forts at Whitehaven. The *Friendship*, on her 1761 tobacco voyage, carried 18 guns and a crew of 28 men.

The seamen who sailed the collier vessels were always in fear of being seized by the press gangs for service in the Royal Navy. When men were being pressed in Dublin, the sailors refused to leave Whitehaven, and when the gangs were active in Whitehaven, they left the area and hid until they were able to obtain a 'Protection'. This was a document issued by the Admiralty which exempted sailors from the attentions of the press gangs. The fear of forced recruitment into the Royal Navy represented a real threat in the lives of the local seamen, as two press gangs with a regulating officer were stationed both in Whitehaven and Dublin throughout most of the 18th century. However, it must be said that the Lowthers were most assiduous in attending at the Admiralty in order to obtain Protections for the men.

During the 1740s and 1750s, which were prosperous years for Whitehaven, the capacity of the Harbour was greatly increased by the building of the Old (Merchants) and the New Tongues. These were years in which there was often a shortage of shipping for the coal trade, and the enhanced facilities greatly reduced the turn round time of the ships.

After 1745, exports of coal again increased steadily and reached 110,000 average tons per annum by 1750. The ships in use at the time were rather larger than those in service in 1700, but to move this quantity of coal required approximately 140-145 ships, making between them perhaps 725 sailings in the year. When the number of ships departing for Virginia, the Baltic and other destinations is added, it is quite clear that Whitehaven, although never a large harbour, was certainly a busy one. The preponderance of coal ships also explains why Sir James Lowther and the Trustees concentrated on the development of the inner Harbour, rather than on the provision of deep-water berths.

In terms of population, Dublin at this time was the second largest city in Britain after London, and was still growing. This was reflected in the continuing increase in the demand for coal, but in the second half of the century Whitehaven's share of the market began to decline. In 1700 Whitehaven supplied 75-80 per cent of all Ireland's coal imports, and was still sending 70 per cent in 1740. However, the proportion had fallen to only 28 per cent by 1790. In 1800, 35 per cent of Ireland's coal was imported from South Wales and Lancashire, and in addition large tonnages were shipped from Maryport, Workington and Harrington. The combined total of tonnages shipped from these latter ports exceeded the tonnage shipped from Whitehaven for the first time in 1790, and Whitehaven's proportion continued to decline thereafter.

This does not mean that the tonnages from Whitehaven actually fell at least not until the 1790s. Over the 30 years 1750 to 1780, exports rose very slowly, the average annual tonnage increasing from 110,000 to 125,000 over the period. During Bateman's first stewardship of the Whitehaven collieries, in the 1780s, annual exports averaged 130,000 tons, and in the one year 1785 exceeded 159,000 tons. However, in the 1790s under Thomas Wylie, shipments to Ireland were much reduced, reaching only 95,000 tons in 1799.

In mid-century, in view of the growing competition from other coalfields, attempts were made to reduce Whitehaven's dependence on the Irish market. John Spedding, on occasion finding that mine output exceeded shipped tonnage, tried for instance to obtain contracts to supply coals to the naval dockyards at Portsmouth and Plymouth. Meantime Sir James Lowther attempted to develop exports to France and Spain, sending coal as ballast in tobacco ships bound for France. Unfortunately both these schemes were unsuccessful. Sir James was keen also to obtain a share of the London market and, although coals were sent there for many years, the tonnages were only very small indeed.

Immediately before the American War of Independence, some coal was going to Virginia and to other colonies in America and, after the war started, to the British forces employed there. The results of the many attempts to penetrate alternative markets were very disappointing, caused mainly by the ships' masters who consistently refused to be diverted from Dublin. Although coals were sent to many destinations, the aggregate tonnage was never more than a very small fraction of that exported to Ireland.

Shipments of coal were again seriously disrupted during the American War of Independence. Whitehaven lost almost 100 ships, commandeered, captured or sunk. American privateers, lying in wait in the Irish Sea, captured several Whitehaven collier ships, and demanded as much as £500 in ransom for their return. Lacking naval escorts, some of the local ships were armed with cannons supplied by Spedding and Co., Seaton Ironworks. Sir James Lowther (later the Earl of Lonsdale) offered to fit out a 74-gun warship of his own, but the war ended before this project could be put in hand.

The development of the coal trade and of the Harbour were inextricably linked throughout the 18th century. The piers, with the exception of the New Pier, were built to handle exports of coal and, as the coal trade expanded, additional facilities were added to accommodate the increased number of ships required. Imports, and exports of goods other than coal, were dealt with at the New Pier and the Old Tongue.

The Ton

When considering coal movements during the 18th century, it is necessary to define the word 'ton'. The ton at this time was a measure of volume, not of weight. The Whitehaven Harbour Act of 1708 defines the ton loaded on to a ship as 192 gallons. This complicated system of measurement was a constant source of dispute between buyer and seller, but it was in use until 1836, when it was made obsolete by the introduction of accurate weighing machines, and the universal acceptance of a standard system of weights and measures.

Cases for Turns of Coal Ships

Ships turns at the coal staithes at Whitehaven were allocated in order of the ships' passing the Sound of the Calf of Man on their outward journey to Dublin, and not on the homeward run.

Directions for the Turn of Coal Ships According to the Several Cases Following, as agreed on by Sir James Lowther and the Masters of Ships—October 1724

CASE 1   Ships loading Coals at Whitehaven and discharging at Dublin, or any other place on the coast of Ireland, in St George's Channel to the Northwards of Tuskar, or Southwards of Rothlins, and return from thence directly in Ballast or with Goods (and Merchandize) either part or full loaded—Are to take their Turns as outward bound to Dublin from the opening of the Sound of the Calf of Man.

CASE 2   Ships loading Coals at Whitehaven, discharging at Dublin, or any other place in the Channel, and taking in Goods for Whitehaven—Also to have Turns as outward to Dublin from the opening of the Calf.

CASE 3   Ships loading Coals at Whitehaven, discharging part thereof at Dublin or some other place in the Channel, and proceeding with the rest to another place in Great Britain, France or Ireland, and then returning to Whitehaven with a part or full loading of Goods or in Ballast—Are to take Turns as Cases 1 & 2.

CASE 4   Ships loading Coals at Whitehaven, discharging their Cargoes without the limits of the Channel in Great Britain, France or Ireland, and bringing back Goods or returning to Whitehaven in Ballast—Are to have the Privilege of Bonded Ships to the West of England.

CASE 5   Ships in the last Case returning to Dublin, Isle of Man, or any other place in the Channel, and from thence bringing back Goods or returning to Whitehaven in Ballast—Are notwithstanding to have the Privilege of Bonded Ships.

CASE 6   Ships in the 4th Case taking Freight for Holland, Norway or other places beyond the Seas—Are to take Turns from the opening of the Red Banks homewards.

CASE 7   Ships loading Coals at Whitehaven and going Coastwise or to the Isle of Man, so that they open not ... the Sound of the Calf—Are ...

CASE 8   New Ships built at Whitehaven and going Coastwise—Are to reckon their Turn from the Time of Launching.

CASE 9   Ships overhauled at Whitehaven, and Ships not trading for a time and then fitting out again, may load as soon as they are ready.

CASE 10   Ships overhauled or New Ships coming from other Places—Are to take Turn from the opening of the Red Banks homewards.

CASE 11   Ships loading Coals at Whitehaven, discharging in Ireland, and then proceeding to any part of America, Norway, Holland or to the South of Cape Finisterre—Are to take Turns from the opening of the Red Banks homewards.

CASE 12   Such Ships at their return, not discharging their Cargoes at Whitehaven, but at Lancaster, Liverpool etc on the Coast of England, or at Glasgow, Kirkcudbright etc in Scotland—Are to take their Turn from the opening of the Red Banks in their Return Home from the place of their Discharge.

CASE 13   Whether Ships may lye at Parton and be admitted to take their Turns at Whitehaven, not having traded in the meantime—Agreed they may, for Both Harbours, and the Shipping of both Harbours to be upon an equal footing.

CASE 14   Ships taking part or their full Loading of Merchandize at Whitehaven, Parton, or Workington, and discharging the same in the Channel, and then bringing back Merchandize or returning to Whitehaven in Ballast—Are to take Turns as outward bound Ships from the opening of the Sound of Calf. Workington Ships to have the same Privilege at Whitehaven as they give to the Whitehaven and Parton Ships, when they go to Workington to load—Agreed to. Note—The Channel above mentioned is understood to be bounded between Roughlins.

CASE 15   Ships loading Coals at Whitehaven, discharging the same at Dublin or any other Place in the Channel, and then proceeding to some other Place and there taking in Goods for Whitehaven. or returning thither in Ballast—Are to take Turns as outward bound from opening out of the Sound of the Calf.

CASE 16   Ships trading to the Northwards with Goods or Merchandize and not opening out of the Sound of the Calf—Are to take their Turns of loading Coals from their arrival at Whitehaven, next after the Ships that have opened out of the Sound of the Calf.

CASE 17   In the last Case as Case 15, Ships discharging their Coals without the limits of the Channel—To have the Privilege of Bonded Ships.

Whitehaven—24 October 1728

Whereas the High Prices of Oats or other Grain in this Town make it necessary to encourage the Importation of them from other Places, Mr Lowther does hereby give Notice that all Ships and Vessels that will give Security to discharge their Coals in the West of England or in Wales, where Corn may be bought at very moderate Rates, shall according to the Rules formally made, have liberty to Load out preferable to all other Ships, and Also at their Return be allowed to Load out immediately for Dublin. Also that all Ships and Vessels whatsoever arriving in the Harbour, and bringing at least one half of their Loading, the said Ships shall be able to carry in Corn, and discharge the same here, and shall have the Privilege immediately to Load out with Coals. This to be made a Standing Rule and Order whenever Oats shall sell for above Five Shillings the Bushel in Whitehaven Market.

Other Exports

At the time that the coal trade was expanding so rapidly, Whitehaven unfortunately lacked most of the basic requirements for the stimulation of economic growth. Not being on a river, there was no primary source of power to drive machinery and, although a few windmills were in use in the town, these were for local use only, as the windmill could not be adapted for large scale operations. An abundance of coal was available, of course, but before the advent of the steam engine, this could be used in coal-burning industries only.

Attempts were made therefore to start businesses for the manufacture of products such as glass bottles, bricks, salt and copperas (sulphate of iron, or green vitriol, used for dyes and ink). These businesses were only partially successful, due largely to the lack of marketing skills. When communications were so poor, and isolated as it was in west Cumberland, Whitehaven was too far distant from the markets where manufactured goods could be sold. The glass bottle works, for instance, might have had more success if the owners had established a presence in some of the large centres of population, particularly in London.

The town was situated in a sparsely populated area which was unable to supply a numerous workforce. Throughout most of the period there was a shortage of labour to man the ships and the businesses which sprang up in support of the mining and shipping interests. Skilled men were reluctant to come to Whitehaven because of insufficient financial incentives and an almost total lack of credit facilities.

Most importantly perhaps, Whitehaven was short of entrepreneurs with skills and access to the capital necessary to start businesses. Sir James Lowther could have filled this role, but chose instead to direct all his energies into trying to gain a monopoly in the local coal industry. It is true that he offered to lend money to local men for business purposes, but the industries were required to be coal orientated, and the amounts offered rarely exceeded 10 per cent of the necessary capital. Known by his contemporaries as 'Farthing Jimmy', Sir James was notorious for his parsimony and, although 'the richest commoner in England', would not invest his money in any business which did not further his ambitions in respect of the coal industry.

However, several businesses were set up specifically to manufacture goods for export to the colonies, but they were only on a small scale and, because of the constraints could not be developed into the substantial businesses such as those that were being created in Lancashire and elsewhere. As a consequence, there was never a ready supply at Whitehaven of manufactured goods for export cargoes, even though at the time there was a very large demand in the West Indies and the American colonies for goods of all descriptions. In the early part of the century, ships left Whitehaven for Virginia carrying clothing (shoes, hats, stockings, and gloves), materials (silk, linen, and woollen), spirits, and metal goods. Some of these items were obtained locally, but goods were obtained from all over the region; from Dumfries, Penrith, Kendal, Cockermouth and Egremont.

Some goods, such as ropes and copperas were supplied by firms which had started as ancillary to the shipping and mining industries. Some woollen cloth, and later linen, was obtained from a small factory at Lowther near Penrith, started by Henry 3rd Viscount Lonsdale, a somewhat distant relative of Sir James Lowther.

Some iron ore was also exported from Whitehaven towards the end of the 17th century and during the early years of the 18th. The ore was mined in the Egremont area, and was exported to Ireland, Scotland and to the Duddon furnace. A staithe was erected on the West Wharf to handle the material, but the trade ceased in the 1720s due to competition from elsewhere. The iron ore staithes, referred to as a landmark in the description of the Harbour, were demolished in the 1730s to make room for the coal staithes. Later in the century, iron ore mined at Frizington was again exported for shipment to Shropshire.

As the century progressed, industry developed near Liverpool and Glasgow, which because of the lower transport costs involved were able to become dominant in the export trades. Whitehaven continued for many years with small scale specialist goods. When he was bankrupted in 1763, Peter How, the town's leading merchant, was found to have creditors from a very large area who had supplied him with goods for export.

Some Whitehaven ships, in search of cargoes, called at ports in southern Ireland, where linen and leather goods were available. Some ships arrived in Virginia carrying goods not from Britain but from the West Indies. The brig *Friendship* for instance, on its annual voyage for tobacco, arrived at Hampton, Virginia on 7 May 1761 loaded with 270 hogsheads of rum and 189 barrels of sugar, which had been picked up in Barbados. Goods of every description were exported through Whitehaven Harbour. It is not possible to provide a comprehensive list, but it would include clothing, furniture, furnishings, paper, pottery, leather goods, metal articles and utensils and so on. Quantities, however, were always small.

Imports

Tobacco

Tobacco was the most important commodity imported through Whitehaven during the 18th century. It was grown principally in Virginia, but also in Maryland, two of the British American colonies. The first Whitehaven vessel known to have crossed the Atlantic in search of tobacco was the *Resolution* in 1683. The master of this vessel was the father of Richard Kelswick, who became one of the town's leading tobacco merchants. Over the following 10 years, *Resolution* made seven voyages to Virginia, and its owners shared profits of £1,200. Sir John Lowther held a one-eighth share in this vessel. Between 1693 and 1707 the trade increased rapidly, about twenty ships being involved and bringing on average 1.5 million pounds of tobacco each year. The volume of the trade was sufficient to justify an additional customs house official because of 'the increase of our plantation trade'.

The English tobacco trade was very severely affected by the Union with Scotland in 1707, when Glasgow merchants were able to intervene. Whitehaven was especially badly affected, and in 1711 only 11 ships entered the Harbour, imports being reduced to about half the 1707 level. The trade recovered only slowly and it was not until 1725 that imports returned to the pre-Union levels; indeed Whitehaven ships were sometimes hired to carry tobacco to Glasgow! During these earlier stages of the trade, most of the tobacco was re-exported from Whitehaven mainly to Dublin, but also to the Isle of Man and Norway.

By 1730, tobacco imports were in the region of two million pounds per annum, at which time the merchants began to exploit the markets of Holland and France. Because of the Navigation Laws of 1660 and 1671, goods from and to the colonies had to be carried in English ships and, from the passing of these Acts, the Dutch had bought their tobacco in England, taking half of the re-exports from Whitehaven in the late 17th century. In the mid-1730s the merchants gained a large share of this market, and in 1740 Holland took four million pounds of the 5.2 million re-exported.

The tobacco trade increased at a phenomenal rate during the 1740s when France began to increase its purchases from Britain. Whitehaven took advantage of this opportunity and, in 1743, 10 million pounds of tobacco were re-exported, 5.5 million to France, 3.5 million to Holland and the remaining million to Ireland. In the mid-1740s, Whitehaven imported more tobacco than Glasgow, Liverpool and Bristol, only London importing more. One-third of all the tobacco imported by the four major ports on the west coast came in through Whitehaven. The peak was reached in 1748 when 10.6 million pounds of tobacco were imported. With good reason John Spedding was able to describe the trade as 'the very life and soul of Whitehaven'. At this period the tobacco merchants were agitating for improvements in the Harbour for their ships, while Spedding was experiencing great difficulty in finding sufficient ships for the coal trade to Ireland.

The trade was in the hands perhaps, of two dozen Whitehaven merchants, among them Peter How, Richard Kelswick, Walter Lutwidge, Thomas Hartley, James (son of John) Spedding, William Hicks, Thomas Patrickson, John Younger and Edward Tubman. All these and many of the others served as Trustees of the Town and Harbour around the middle years of the century.

13   The 'Love' Bowl.

By 1750, the peak had passed. The Glasgow merchants, amidst allegations of customs irregularities, were importing 60 per cent more than their counterparts in West Cumberland. The Whitehaven tobacco trade, although at smaller volumes, continued successfully during the 1750s and into the 1760s. The vessel *Friendship*, after delivering its cargo of rum and sugar to Virginia in 1761, returned to Whitehaven carrying 424 hogsheads of tobacco, 28 tons of pig iron and several thousand barrel staves. Its return cargo on the 1763 voyage consisted of 406 hogsheads of tobacco, 16 tons of pig iron, 5,000 barrel staves, 200 feet of plank, and '2 caskes Snakeroot'.

At the end of the Seven Years' War with France, Peter How, Whitehaven's leading merchant, was declared bankrupt. He had been heavily involved in the tobacco trade with France, and the difficulties experienced in trading during the war were a major

Sale of Tobacco.

TO be SOLD, at Mrs. HAYTON's *Assembly Room*, in *Howgill-street*, WHITEHAVEN, on WEDNESDAY the 15th of APRIL, inst. a Parcel of

GOOD VIRGINIA TOBACCO.

In excellent Condition. A CATALOGUE will be ready to deliver on MONDAY the 13th inst. Bills drawn by the *Newcastle, Leeds, York, Manchester, Liverpool*, and *Glasgow* Bankers, payable in London at Three Months Date, will suit the Seller, and be accepted in Payment.

Such Buyers as chuse to pay in Gold will be allowed the Discount for that Period of Time, at the Common Interest. All Tobacco bought for Exportation must be shipped off in one Month. No Advance of the Duty in the Export Tobacco will be required.

The Catalogues will contain Weights, Allowances, &c. &c.
JOHN WILSON, Broker.

☞ Samples to be seen by applying to SAMUEL MARTIN, Esq. in *Lowther-street*.
Whitehaven. April 6th, 1778.

14   Advertisement from the *Cumberland Pacquet*, 7 April 1778. Although Whitehaven's tobacco trade had virtually ceased by this time, occasional cargoes still entered the port.

factor in his failure. By the late 1770s, tobacco imports into Whitehaven were about one-third of the level reached in the late 1740s, and represented only six per cent of the imports of the four west coast ports, compared with the 33 per cent attained 30 years previously.

The American War of Independence finally brought about the end of the Whitehaven tobacco trade. The Americans took over the shipment of tobacco, trading with Bristol, Liverpool and Glasgow, with the result that the Whitehaven merchants ceased to trade and were bankrupted. Many of the merchants had made investments in plantations in Virginia, but these were lost at the end of the war. The estates of Samuel Martin, for example, were confiscated without compensation by the State Government of Virginia.

Obviously the tobacco trade was extremely important in the economy of Whitehaven during the 18th century. Most of the merchants had made considerable fortunes, much of which, in order to establish their status, was invested in land and property. Unfortunately, the trade did not last long enough and declined too rapidly for them to make a serious attempt to use their wealth in the development of manufacturing industries in the region. By the end of the century the trade had ceased and Whitehaven Harbour was left almost completely dependent on the coal and shipping industries.

Other Imports

The importation of goods and commodities other than tobacco into Whitehaven cannot be disregarded.

During the 17th century, a coastal trade was developed, coal and salt being exchanged for grain. The increasing population of Whitehaven created a demand for more food, and grain imports became a significant feature of the trade of the Harbour throughout the 18th century. Following several poor harvests in the 1720s, and food riots in the town in 1728, John Spedding established a granary in Lowther Street in 1731 in which the imported grain was stored. There the grain was held until the local price rose above a given level—for many years 4s. 6d. per bushel—when it was then released at that price to workmen on the Lowther payroll. Preference was given to men using their own horses in their work, but the Spedding Brewery Company also received favourable terms. By holding down grain prices in this way, the practical John Spedding considered that he would be able to refuse demands for higher wages which he would then have been unable to reduce when grain prices had returned to a more normal level.

Much of the grain, wheat, barley and oats, was brought from Wales, usually from the ports of Haverfordwest, Milford Haven and Carmarthen, although some was also purchased in Dumfries. Some grain, mainly barley, was probably shipped from London, as several public houses in Whitehaven advertised their home-brewed beer as being 'made from the finest Hertfordshire barley'. Several of the Whitehaven merchants, including Peter How, Thomas Patrickson and James Spedding, used their ships in this trade, but much of the grain was carried in Welsh ships skippered by Welsh masters. Sir James Lowther was also involved, using ships over which he had control, in the importation of hay, beans and oats, which were sold to Spedding for use as animal fodder.

A glance at the list of imports subject to the payment of harbour dues will show that wines and spirits played a significant role in Whitehaven trade. French wines and brandy were imported in the 1680s from Bordeaux, and continued until the 1720s, when the trade fell away because of increases in customs duties and also because of a high level of smuggling. However, wines and spirits were still being imported late in the century when Robert Jefferson founded a business which still survives in the late 20th century. The principal customer of the importers was Sir James Lowther, whose cellars at both Whitehaven and Lowther were kept stocked from these sources.

A very significant volume of trade was generated by the Whitehaven merchants with the Baltic area. As the Harbour developed, a greater number of ships was required, thereby creating a demand for ship-building materials. Trading began in the 1680s, when timber, tar, sails and hemp were imported. During the 18th century, the growing ship-building and rope-making businesses were heavily dependent on materials imported from the Baltic countries, and the trade grew, in terms of volume and value, to an importance second only to that of tobacco. At its peak, about twenty ships sailed for the Baltic each year. Much of this business was carried on by Thomas Patrickson and Thomas Hartley, who imported materials for use in their own businesses. Patrickson was a partner in the Patrickson-Spedding ship-building company, while Hartley made ropes for use in both the shipyards and in the coal mines.

Quantities of iron were also brought from the Baltic for use in the many smithies in Whitehaven, and also to be used in the manufacture of goods for export to the West Indies and the American colonies.

The importance to Whitehaven of these commodities from the Baltic is clearly shown by their inclusion in the 1708 list of goods subject to payment of harbour dues. Many other goods were imported into Whitehaven, of course. Most of them were either food and drink for immediate consumption, or were materials for use in businesses ancillary to the shipbuilding and coal industries.

Chapter 5

The Coal Staithes and Hurries,
and the Fortifications

As the coal pits nearest to the Harbour became worked out in the early part of the 18th century, it became necessary to mine further afield. Because of the lack of roads, transporting the coals became difficult and expensive. Packhorses were used for many years, but in the 1720s John Spedding began to examine the use of overground railways.

Sir James Lowther had taken leases on mines at Seaton, near Workington, and in 1732 he built the first such railway in Cumberland, a wooden waggonway connecting the pits to Workington Harbour. Its success determined that similar waggonways should be built at Whitehaven. Corporal and Swinburn pits were first connected to the Harbour, and a little later a second waggonway was built from Saltom Pit. The two ways delivered the coals to a staithe or gallery at the Harbour side. The purpose of the staithe was to facilitate the loading of ships, and also to provide storage for coals when ships were not available for loading. Work began on the staithe in 1732, when the Trustees' minutes recorded the exchange of several small parcels of land along the West Wharf, and was completed in the following year.

The working of the whole operation is best described in a paper published in 1801 as part of a biography of William Brownrigg MD FRS, written by his colleague Joshua Dixon MD.

> The coals are conveyed to the ships by a very ingenious contrivance which was first practiced by Mr Carlisle Spedding. Frames of wood are placed, in an exactly parallel line, along the road, leading from the pits; which has an uninterrupted declevity, though in some parts it is scarce perceptible. The loaden waggon is carried upon these frames down the inclined plane, not by the labour of horses, or of men, but according to a simple law in mechanics, by its own weight. The occasional assistance of one man is necessary, to prevent the waggon from acquiring too great a velocity, in consequence of a quick descent of the road. This is performed by two levers, connected with the first pair of wheels: the friction of which regulates their motion: and as the power is applied at a distance, an inconsiderable exertion is sufficient for the purpose.

In the Howgill Colliery, the waggons proceed in this manner, until they arrive at a covered gallery made of wood, which is elevated about 37 feet above the level of the quay. From this gallery, the necessary supply of coals is obtained, by means of spouts. Five of these are fixed, at an angle of about 45 degrees; and so conveniently distant from each other, that 5 vessels, of very considerable burthen may be loaded at one tide, under them. The bottom of the waggon being opened, the coals run with great rapidity, down the spouts to the ship. When there are no vessels ready to receive the coals, they are dropped, through holes, left in the gallery, into the magazine; the bottom of which is about 25 feet below the gallery or waggonway. The waggons are again filled with these coals in the following summer months, when an increase in the trade requires them.

The waggonway on which the coals are carried into the magazine, and to the different spouts, has a descent, from the entrance to the place where the waggons pass out of about 1/8th of an inch in each yard.

Dr. Dixon goes on to describe the circuitous route by which the waggons, under gravity and assisted by turnrails, pass through and eventually emerge from the gallery,

where a horse waits for each waggon, to draw it up the hill, a little to the south-east of the bowling green. In this situation the main and bye waggonways lie adjoining each other.

The covered part of the magazine, placed parallel to the quay is, in length 115 yards; in breadth 19 yards, and in depth below the waggonway 8 yards. The uncovered part is at the south end 40 yards long; 28 yards broad and 7 yards deep.

The staithe was capable of holding 3,000 waggon loads of coal, or about 6,500 tons.

The structure was obviously of enormous size, occupying as it did practically the whole length of the West Wharf, and must have dominated the Harbour scene. It was regarded as one of the wonders of the age, and many people visited Whitehaven to see it, and to listen to the thunderous noise of the coals rushing down the hurries into the holds of the ships. Although much repaired, the staithes and hurries were still in use into the 19th century.

Coals from pits that were not connected to the waggonways were brought to the Harbour throughout the 18th century by horse and cart, and it was not until 1803, when Bransty Arch was at last brought into operation, that a staithe was built near the North East Wall for the loading of ships with coals from the Whingill Colliery.

The waggonways and staithes were a very much quicker and cheaper method of transporting coals from pit to ships than the use of horses and carts carrying sacks, and were a major contributing factor enabling Lowther to gain a commanding lead in the Cumberland coal trade.

15 Bransty Arch. It was intended by Carlisle Spedding that the arch would form part of the Whingill Waggonway. Erection began in 1755, but it was not completed until 1802. The waggons ran from left to right across the arch, the North Harbour being immediately behind the buildings on the right.

The Fortifications

During the 18th century, many of the harbours of Britain, including Whitehaven, were fortified to protect shipping and port facilities in case of attack from the sea. The fortification of Whitehaven began at the time of the English Civil War, for in 1639 Sir Christopher Lowther bought 'two pieces of ordinance' and proposed to 'make a fortification for them on the peere'.

Little is known of further developments until the early years of the 18th century, when reference is made in the description of the boundaries of Whitehaven Harbour in the Act of 1708 to 'the Platform' at the landward end of the Old Pier, the place where cannons were mounted.

The earliest reference to the subject in the minutes of the Harbour Trustees occurs in August 1740 when it was ordered 'that Seven Guns of Four Pound Shot be added to the Great Guns upon the Battery and that Sir James Lowther purchase same, together with a Parcel of Shot, Rammers, Sponges etc.'.

The treasurer's accounts for the six years ending 25 March 1746 show 'Charge of the Battery, Guns Arms, Powder etc. £1121.18. 8.'. This was the period during which the Old Fort and Lunette Battery were built as protection from the French, who had declared war on Britain in 1744 during the War of the Austrian Succession.

The period of the Second Jacobite Rebellion was a time of great stress in Whitehaven, for in June 1746 it is recorded that the Trustees had been put to great expense, in gaining Intelligence of the Motions of the Rebel Armies in their several Marches Southward and return to Scotland, in assisting to reduce the garrison of Carlisle after it fell into the Hands of the Rebels, in carrying off to sea the Large and Small Cannon and Military Stores of all kinds ... and in divers other Services whereby the Peace of the Town has been happily preserved and the Rebels frustrated in their Wicked Designs of plundering the Town and Neighbourhood ...

The cost of these activities totalled £478 18s. 5d. which included £17 2s. 6d. 'paid by order to the Gunner of the Fort, for his salary for Three Quarters and Charges of Oiling the Great Guns'.

In 1762, at the time of the Seven Years' War with France, the strength of the defences of Whitehaven was again under review as there is a reference to

John Wooler Esq. having pursuant to an order from the Board of Ordnance made a Survey of the Harbour of Whitehaven, Forts, and Coasts adjacent in order to erect further Forts, Platforms and other Works necessary for the reception of the Guns and Stores his Majesty has been graciously pleased to order to be sent here for the Defence of the Town and Harbour from any attempts that may be made thereon by the Enemy in time of War, this day delivered his Report to the Trustees, together with the Plans of the Buildings to be erected necessary for the Reception of the said Guns and Stores and for the further Protection and Security of the Town and Harbour. Ordered that the said Plans be laid before Sir James Lowther Bart. and Gentlemen of the Town for their Consideration, in order to be carried into execution with all convenient speed, and that Estimates be made of the Charge and Expence of erecting the said Work.

The Trustees returned thanks to the Board of Ordnance and also to Mr. Wooler to whom they gave '25 Guineas as a present for his Trouble, Journey and Expences hereabouts'.

It is possible that some new guns were added to the Old Fort and to the Lunette Battery, but it is clear that no new works were commenced. The war with France ended early in 1763, and the danger passed; the Trustees on 21 March 1763 ordered:

that the Guns in the Lunette Battery be dismounted, and properly laid on Beds, the Carriages put into the Storehouse and that two of the Six Pounders be removed from the Old Fort to the Lunette Battery, and then mounted, that the ten Eighteen Pounders be likewise dismounted and properly laid on Beds, and the Carriages put into the Storehouse. That the Forty two and Twenty four Pounders be placed on Beds under the Shed in the Harbour Yard, and the Carriages put into the Storehouse, and that such of the Stores as can be put into the Storehouse be placed there and all the Guns and Carriages that want painting be sufficiently painted.

The defences of the Harbour were in this semi-dismantled state when the famous raid was carried out in 1778 by John Paul Jones (see Chapter VI). The Trustees then hastily revived Mr. Wooler's report of 1762 and on 23 June 1778 recorded:

> ... having formerly at the Expence of the Harbour erected Forts and Batteries on the West side thereof and others being thought necessary to be erected on the North east side of the said Harbour, have resolved to petition the Secretary of State to request that His Majesty will be pleased to give Directions to Erect a Fort or Battery upon the Strand at Bransty near Jack a Dandy Hill as projected, at the Expences thereof Estimated in August 1762 by Mr John Wooler, an Engineer then sent from Clifford's Fort ... and also to supply the said Fort with such a number of Cannon, Stores and Mattrosses, and so many Stand of Small Arms as His Majesty shall think proper to order.

This was followed in September 1778 by an order from the Trustees:

> that the Six Forty two Pound Cannon now lying in the Harbour Yard shall be mounted on Wooden Platforms at the following places viz;- Three upon the Hill on the South west side of the Harbour near the Bowling Green, and Three upon the Hill at Redness on the North east side of the Harbour, and that a Temporary Guard House and Magazine be erected at each of the above places.

Both of the 1778 proposals were proceeded with, although at a leisurely pace, for it was not until November 1788 that the guns were mounted in the new forts and test firing began. The firing of the cannons resulted in many broken windows in neighbouring houses, the occupants of which sought recompense from the Trustees. Bills paid on 2 December 1788 show some of the costs of this exercise.

Hire of Labour mounting the guns	3	4	10
Hire of Cartmen for Carriage of the guns	1	9	8
Repairs of Broken Windows (7 names)	4	13	11

In 1793, Britain was again at war, with Revolutionary France, and the defences of Whitehaven were again put on the alert. The guns in the Old Fort and the Lunette Battery were mounted and put in good order, ready for immediate use: 'Fram'd work be got ready to Form Embrazures, to be filled with Clay and Straw well wrought for that purpose, and to be six and a half feet high from the Platform'. The guns at the other emplacements were also put in readiness. It seems that little attention had been given to the fortifications since the building of the new batteries only two or three years previously.

The authorities must have have thought that Whitehaven was in imminent danger, because at the same time Lord Lonsdale ordered that the arms of the Cumberland Militia should be deposited in the fort at Whitehaven, and under the guard room in the fort, 'and the Key might be delivered to the Serjeant Major of the Cumberland Militia'.

Again, in 1797, the guns were put in readiness, 'in consequence of several Letters received in Town that the Enemy have landed on the Coast of Pembrokeshire'. Sods were cut on Whillymoor for making embrazures at the forts, a 'Night Patrole' was started in Whitehaven, and four 18-pounders were sent to St Bees for additional defence. The Trustees appropriated £100 from the Voluntary Fund to cover the expenses.

Corporal McDougal of the Invalid Battalion, Royal Artillery, and two gunners arrived in Whitehaven to inspect the guns and put them in order. McDougal's report indicated a great deal of neglect and a shortfall in equipment. All the guns and carriages needed painting and oiling, while the ammunition stocks were short of 2,799 wads, 779 cartridges, 108 round shot and 80 barrels of gunpowder, among many other items. The shortages of equipment included eight straps with buckles, two Hanoverian trucks, one dozen sheepskins, and three frocks 'for himself and the 2 privates'. The Trustees' minutes do not indicate what remedial action, if any, was taken.

The guns taken to St Bees were there for about eighteen months on the land of one John Richardson. A party, sent by the Trustees to bring back the guns to Whitehaven, was unable to gain access to the land, as Richardson had locked the gate pending receipt of payment for damage done to the land. The party, on its way back to Whitehaven empty handed, was intercepted by the Rev. C.C. Church who, on discovering their business, stated that 'no one would fetch away the guns, until he, Church, had an order from His Majesty'!

Magazines for the storage of gunpowder were not provided. In order to minimise the risk of accidental explosion, powder was lodged in the cellars of various tradesmen in the town, and periodically calls were made for small quantities to be delivered to the several forts.

The guns supplied to Whitehaven over the years were of various calibres. Between 1740 and 1778, the guns at the Old Fort and the Lunette Battery consisted of a mixture of four, six, 18, 24, and 42 pounders although the 24s and 42s were kept in store after 1763. According to the *Parson and White Directory* of 1829, several 32 and 36 pounders arrived from Woolwich after the raid by John Paul Jones in 1778.

The number of guns at any one time is not easy to ascertain but it seems unlikely that there were ever more than 35 or 36, some of which would be unserviceable. The claim by John Paul Jones that he spiked 36 cannons in the fort and battery would appear to be highly exaggerated, as it seems that the Fort usually had eight or nine guns and the Lunette Battery nine, although of small calibre. The report in *Parson and White* (1829) states that the newly-arrived cannons brought the total to 98, but this must be an error, as *Mannex and Whelan* (1847) gives a total of 43, 13 of which could not be used, as forming the defences of the Harbour shortly after 1800. By 1800, all the guns were 18 pounders or bigger, so it was probably during the 1790s that some of the smaller guns were sunk into the quays of the Harbour to be used as mooring posts.

Apart from the few shots fired at the retreating John Paul Jones, the guns at Whitehaven were never fired in anger. Occasionally, test firing was carried out but, except during periods of national emergency, the fortifications were maintained at a minimum level.

Chapter 6

John Paul Jones and the Raid on Whitehaven

Probably the most dramatic event in the history of Whitehaven occurred in the early hours of 23 April 1778 when John Paul Jones carried out an armed raid on the Harbour.

John Paul—he did not add the name Jones until 1773—was born the son of a gardener at Arbigland in the parish of Kirkbean, near Dumfries on 7 July 1747. At an early age, he decided he wanted to go to sea and at 13 was sent to Whitehaven where he was apprenticed to Mr. John Younger, a merchant trading with the West Indies and Virginia.

John Paul sailed almost immediately in a Whitehaven vessel, the *Friendship* (brig 179 tons, Capt. Robert Benson) and, after calling at Barbados, arrived at Hampton, Virginia on 7 May 1761. The ship returned to Whitehaven in the autumn, and the voyage was repeated in 1762 and 1763, returning with cargoes of tobacco and timber. During these voyages young Paul studied navigation and other subjects connected with his chosen profession, and although only a boy became quite skilled.

On his return from the 1763 voyage, he discovered that Mr. Younger had become bankrupt. Younger therefore released John Paul from his indentures and helped him to obtain the appointment of third mate of the *King George* of Whitehaven, a purpose-built slave ship. Paul sailed on one complete voyage with the *King George* in 1764/5 and, although engaged for a second, he left the ship in Jamaica.

John Paul visited Whitehaven only five or six times between voyages, but he became acquainted with many of the townspeople and knew the environs of the Harbour extremely well. During the years 1766-73, John Paul served as captain of several vessels trading with the West Indies. On one voyage aboard the *John of Kirkcudbright*, the ship's carpenter, Mungo Maxwell, was flogged for incompetence and insubordination. Maxwell later died of fever aboard another vessel, but his father insisted that the flogging was the cause of death and, on his return to Kirkcudbright, Paul was held for murder. His reputation suffered severely when word of this incident reached Whitehaven.

On another voyage, this time aboard *Betsy of London*, the crew mutinied in Tobago over arrears of pay. The ringleader aimed a blow with a club at Paul, who ran him through with his sword, killing him instantly. Even though the evidence was obviously in his favour, Paul chose to flee Tobago, and later re-appeared in Virginia where he was known variously as John Jones, Paul Jones, or John Paul Jones.

Relations at this time between Britain and the American colonies were extremely tense, and the possibility of war could not be ruled out. The American Congress decided to create a Continental Navy, for which competent officers were urgently required. John Paul Jones applied for and obtained on 7 December 1775 a commission as first lieutenant in the new navy. He was posted first to the armed ship *Alfred* which flew the 'Grand Union Flag'.

Jones served with some distinction against the British Navy after the outbreak of the American War of Independence in 1776, in command of the sloop *Providence*, but was never popular with the senior commanders. He was of course a Scot with no roots in America but he made known his irritation at being only the 18th in seniority among the ships' captains, and was also over-fond of telling the naval authorities how to run their navy.

Perhaps as a result, Jones was given the command of a warship *Ranger*, which was specially commissioned to carry the news of the surrender of General Burgoyne at Saratoga, to Benjamin Franklin, American Ambassador to France. Jones left Portsmouth, New Hampshire on 1 November 1777, and reached Nantes on 2 December, only to find that a French vessel had arrived with duplicate despatches 24 hours previously.

Jones moved to Brest where he devised a scheme with two objectives in mind. He planned first to raid an English seaport and destroy the shipping there in retaliation for similar raids by the British Navy on the coast of America. His second objective was to capture some important personage to be held as a hostage, in order to force the British Government to exchange Americans taken prisoner. The British Government regarded American sailors as pirates and traitors and refused to acknowledge their rights as belligerents.

Ranger eventually left Brest accompanied by the French frigate *Fortunee* on 10 April 1778 and sailed towards the Irish Sea. After four days, *Fortunee* returned to

16   Bust of John Paul Jones.

Brest, but Jones headed north and on 18 April was off the Point of Ayre, the northern cape of the Isle of Man.

It was essential, of course, to Jones's plan that his whereabouts should remain unknown ashore but, off the coast of the Isle of Man, the *Ranger* was challenged by HM Revenue Cutter *Hussar* from Whitehaven. After a brief engagement, during which *Hussar* received a hit on the stern and holes in her mainsail, the cutter got away and returned to Whitehaven where the captain was able to report the presence of a vessel with hostile intentions.

John Paul Jones decided to carry out his plan for a descent on Whitehaven on 22 April, in order to burn the shipping there. The attack was to be a surprise hit and run raid to inflict as much damage as possible, but the crew of *Ranger* were not at all enthusiastic about the enterprise. They had enlisted in the hope of prize money, but the voyage so far had yielded very little.

The ship's surgeon, Ezra Green, denounced the plan as rash: 'nothing could be got', he said, 'by burning poor people's property'. The first and second lieutenants declined to take part pleading that they were 'overcome by fatigue'. Jones, however, was determined to carry out the raid and, although the response to his call for volunteers was poor, three officers and 29 men agreed to accompany him. One of the volunteers was an Irishman enrolled as David Smith, but also known as David Freeman.

The raid got off to a bad start. Contrary winds delayed *Ranger*'s approach to Whitehaven and at midnight on 22 April she was still some three miles off-shore. However, two boats' crews were made up, with Jones and Lieutenant Meijerin in charge of one, and Lieutenant Samuel Wallingsford of the Marines and Midshipman Ben Hill in charge of the other. The men rowed against an outgoing tide for over three hours, the long pull proving unexpectedly arduous. The men were equipped with pistols and cutlasses and also carried lanterns and a supply of combustible materials.

At the time of the raid, Whitehaven Harbour was defended by the Old Fort situated between the Old and New Piers at their landward ends, and by the Lunette or Half-Moon Battery which was situated some 200 yards away on the beach. Jones's plan was to send Wallingsford into the Harbour to attack the ships moored at the Old (or Merchants') and the New Tongues, while he neutralised the forts, and then attacked the ships in the South Harbour near the coal hurries.

After reaching the New Pier, the boats separated, Wallingsford entering the harbour while Jones landed near the Old Fort. The fort was soon taken, the men standing on each others shoulders to gain entry through the embrasures. Despite the warning given by the captain of the cutter *Hussar*, no sentries were posted and the forts' crew were asleep in the guard room. After capturing the fort, Jones sent his men to set fire to ships in the Harbour, while he, taking only his midshipman Joe Green with him, went off to immobilise the guns in the Lunette Battery. Jones later claimed to have spiked 36 cannons at the two forts.

On returning to the Old Fort, Jones expected to see the shipping in the harbour well ablaze, but in fact there was not a light to be seen, and his men had disappeared. Wallingsford and his crew, to Jones's great astonishment, had abandoned their mission and had come ashore near Old Fort. They explained that they had heard noises ashore which had frightened them, that their candles had gone out, and that in any case nothing was to be gained by burning ships which would deprive the poor of their living (this last from Wallingsford). Jones found his men in a public house at the end of the Old Pier 'making free with the liquor etc'.

Jones was not deterred by the situation, however, although 'the day came on apace, yet I would be no means retreat while any hopes of success remained'. He rallied his men, a light was obtained from the public house, and a fire started on a collier vessel, the *Thompson*, a new ship moored near the coal hurries. She did not burn readily and Jones's men eventually found a barrel of tar to help the blaze.

Unbeknown to Jones, during this part of the raid, the Irishman, David Smith or Freeman, was running through the town rousing the inhabitants and warning them of the danger. Freeman, as he preferred to be called, later admitted that he had enrolled aboard *Ranger* at Portsmouth, New Hampshire in order to obtain a passage back to Ireland.

As a result of Freeman's warning, the townspeople were beginning to stir and, arriving at the Harbour, tackled the blaze aboard *Thompson* which after some endeavour they managed to extinguish. Jones described the scene in his memoirs:

> As it was almost eight o'clock in the morning, and as the inhabitants came running by thousands, I was not able to delay any longer my retreat, which I made in very good order. When all my people had re-embarked, I still remained for some minutes upon the outside mole to observe at my leisure the terror, panic and stupidity of the inhabitants, who in numbers of at least ten thousand remained motionless like statues, or ran hither and thither like madmen to reach the hills on the other side of the town. The retirement had already carried my boats some distance from the shore when the English dared to draw nearer from their fort; finding the cannon spiked there, they brought some pieces from the vessels and fired upon my boats. I answered their salute with several swivel guns which I had placed in the stern of my barge.

Whether Jones's retiral was as leisurely as he implies is doubtful, as are the numbers of guns, ships and people he reports as being deployed against him. However he was soon back on board *Ranger* and sailing north.

The raid on Whitehaven was over. The damage done was inconsequential—the collier *Thompson* was soon repaired and returned to service—but the effect on morale was tremendous. No enemy had set foot on British soil for centuries and the raid spread great alarm. At Whitehaven a public subscription was organised which raised some £850 within four days, the money being used to improve the town's defences. The Cumberland and Westmorland Militia were marched at great pace from Penrith, night patrols were set up in Whitehaven and a 10 p.m. curfew was imposed. Some of the guns from Old Fort were taken and set up on the North Wall to improve the effectiveness of the fortifications.

Their lordships of the Admiralty of course were furious at this slight to the British Navy. Twelve ships were deployed to search the Irish Sea for Jones, but without success. Perhaps most seriously, the raid had the effect of doubling insurance rates for ships and their cargoes. This had a dramatic effect on the Whitehaven merchants trading across the Atlantic, and many ships were lost which had not been insured.

Although the raid on Whitehaven, from Jones's point of view, was not a great success, it must be seen in the larger context of the success achieved during the 28 days of the cruise which began at Brest on 10 April. During the voyage Jones sank three merchantmen, captured two others which were sent back to Brest as prizes, made two armed landings on the British mainland, and defeated in action HMS *Drake*, which was also taken to Brest as a prize.

There was an intriguing incident in Whitehaven immediately after the raid, when John Birkhead, letter carrier to the Post Office, put it about the town that he had delivered a letter addressed to Captain Paul Jones care of Mrs. Sarah Alkin, at the *Grapes* public house in Marlborough Street. Mrs. Alkin protested strongly on the grounds that the story was to the prejudice of her character and also of her business. Birkhead was forced to recant in a letter which was published in the *Cumberland Pacquet* on 27 April 1778.

The career of John Paul Jones did not again affect Whitehaven. After a period as a Rear Admiral in the Russian Navy, he retired to Paris where he died on 18 July 1792, aged 45 years.

Chapter 7

The Spedding Family

No examination of Whitehaven in the 18th century would be complete without some reference to the Spedding family. Members of this family gave almost one hundred years of devoted service to the Lowthers, and held most of the important positions in the local community, making a direct contribution to the development of the Lowther collieries, the Harbour, and local industry.

Edward Spedding, d.1706

Edward Spedding, one of Sir John Lowther's Westmorland tenants, arrived in Whitehaven in the 1680s, where a position in the custom house had been found for him. He also took a lease on a farm at Aikbank, where he supplemented his income by working as a carrier. His efforts, however, were not very well rewarded as, when he died in 1706, his estate was valued at only £17. However he was the father of two of Whitehaven's most eminent men, John and Carlisle Spedding.

John Spedding, 1685-1758

Edward's eldest son John was born in 1685, and entered the service of the Lowthers in 1700 as a 15-year-old domestic servant, with a salary of £10 per annum. His diligence and ability were soon recognised, and he was bequeathed two years' wages in Sir John's will in 1705. Sir John also recommended to his son, Sir James, that young Spedding 'be imployed in controuling the steward's accounts, or otherwise as he shall think fit'. Among his duties he was to watch carefully the activities of John Gale, the Whitehaven colliery steward. It was found that Gale had embezzled a large sum of money and, following reports and complaints by Spedding, Gale was dismissed in 1707 and Spedding was appointed colliery steward in his place.

In this role he was responsible for running the coal mines, keeping detailed accounts of mining costs, and collecting money from the ships' masters. He sent detailed reports on these activities to Sir James, who lived in London, thus beginning a correspondence which continued for almost half a century.

William Gilpin, Lowther's estate steward, retired in 1722, and was succeeded by his son Richard, who had to accept the position jointly with John Spedding. This arrangement was not a success, as Richard Gilpin turned out to be lazy and incompetent, and was removed in 1730. At this juncture, John handed over his position as colliery steward to his brother Carlisle, and took over as principal estate steward, a position he held until his death in 1758.

As estate steward his job was very wide ranging. He collected rents, drew up leases, allocated plots of land in the town to would-be builders, and negotiated with tenants regarding maintenance of buildings. He looked after the domestic arrangements at Whitehaven Castle, and even oversaw the welfare of the fish in the ponds there.

Spedding's main activities, however, were centred on coal. At the time, Lowther was looking for increased output in order to further his aim of gaining a monopoly in the coal trade in West Cumberland. It was thought that the Howgill mines were almost worked out, and consequently Spedding was constantly on the lookout for further coal bearing land. He advised Lowther on which land to buy, and usually carried out the negotiations himself prior to purchase. He was not above resorting to bribery, such as the promise of a job, say as a tidewaiter, nor above using threats, such as the foreclosure of a mortgage to gain his ends. Often, in order that the local landowners were kept unaware of Sir James's interest, land was bought in the name of John Spedding, before later conveyance to Lowther. During Spedding's period of office 79 parcels of land were bought, at a total value of £47,500.

John Spedding was responsible for many innovations in the collieries. He urged Sir James to install the first Newcomen atmospheric engine in the area (in 1716), in order to pump water from the mines. He suggested overground railways as early as 1725, and was eventually responsible for the coal staithes at the Harbour, and the wooden waggonways which connected them to some of the pits which were built during the 1730s. Taken with the work done by his brother Carlisle in improving output from the mines, and also in sinking many new pits, coal output was trebled in the first half of the 18th century.

There can be little doubt that Spedding saw the Harbour as an extension of the coal works. Just as he determined the rates at which the leaders carried coals to the Harbour, so he set the price at which the coal was sold to the ships' masters. He also organised the rota on which the ships were loaded.

From the 1720s attempts were made to establish industries in Whitehaven which would consume coal. Unfortunately, Lowther refused to establish businesses himself, and restricted himself to encouraging others. Attempts were made to start brickworks, potteries, saltpans, naileries, and so on, mostly unsuccessfully and usually because of lack of capital. John Spedding was not one to miss an opportunity to make money for himself, and he became a partner in the Whitehaven Glasshouse Co. formed in 1732, taking a one-eighth share. His fellow shareholders were Sir James Lowther, Thomas Lutwidge, Walter Lutwidge, Abraham Chambers and William Gilpin. The purpose of the company was to export bottles to London and Dublin, but the bottles were found to be faulty in design, being 'weak in the neck an abundance breaking on corking'. The company eventually failed in 1739, the owners losing their capital of £2,400. The glassworks was then let to the Spedding Brothers, who in 1741 and 1742 sent bottles to Belfast, Dublin, Dumfries, Kirkcudbright, Wigton, Carlisle, and Lancaster as well as some as far as Norway. In these two years the Speddings are reputed to have made profits of £1,200-£1,400. The glassworks was closed in 1742.

At an expanding port such as Whitehaven new ships were always required, and in 1732 John set up a shipbuilding company in partnership with his brother Carlisle and Thomas Patrickson. This business was successful, but was restructured in 1748 following the death of Patrickson. John transferred his shares to his son James, while Carlisle divided his shares between himself and his son, also James. A second Thomas Patrickson inherited his father's shares. Among other things, the Patricksons were timber merchants, a commodity for which the shipbuilding company was a favoured customer.

Similarly, Spedding saw a good opportunity in the business of rope making. With Walter Lutwidge, John Hamilton and Joseph Littledale as partners, he opened a rope walk known as Brackenthwaite No 1 in 1727. This firm sold ropes to the Lowther coal mines, as well as to the shipbuilders, and was very successful. From 1746, John Spedding ran the company by himself after a disagreement with Lutwidge, and it was eventually sold by Spedding's executors in 1765 for £1,800.

The Speddings were also involved in a brewery venture. John and Carlisle began the operation in 1743, at a time when John's son James was importing grain into Whitehaven. No doubt malting barley at favourable terms was available to the brewery.

Sir James Lowther, living in London, had to ensure that his views on all matters affecting Whitehaven were known in the area. This task fell to John Spedding. At the time of the scavenger controversy, for instance, John was a member of the Jury of the Court Leet, and was thus able to ensure that the situation was resolved in accordance with Lowther's wishes.

In order to further the Lowther cause, Sir James nominated John Spedding to the first Board of Trustees of the Town and Harbour when it was formed in 1709. He was a member continuously until his death in 1758. He was appointed secretary/treasurer, also in 1709, for which he received a salary. In April 1725 the treasurer was ordered to 'pay his own salary of £5 p.a. for keeping the Harbour Accounts for the last 3 years'. Again, in August 1740, he was awarded a gratuity of £20 'for drawing up Accounts from the commencement of the first Act, and drawing up estimates and papers to be laid before the House of Commons in obtaining The Act 13 Geo II'. At the same time 'Mr Speddings allowance for Registering the Accounts of the Harbour' was increased from £5 to £10 per annum.

On 5 May 1740, John saw his son, Lowther, appointed collector of harbour duties. Unfortunately, Lowther died at the early age of 28 in 1746. He was succeeded as collector by his father, John, whose son James provided the necessary surety of £1,000.

When John Spedding died in 1758, he was succeeded as secretary, treasurer, and collector of duties by his nephew, James, son of Carlisle. James also replaced John as the Lowther nominated Trustee.

It seems reasonable to assume that Sir James consulted with John Spedding when deciding who should be appointed as Trustees of the town and Harbour. Both of John's sons joined the board, Lowther from 1739 to 1746, and James from 1743 to 1758. Carlisle was a Trustee from 1718 until 1755 and Carlisle's son James served from 1758 to 1788. It will be noticed that, once appointed, all the Speddings remained in office until their deaths. It should also be noted that William Brownrigg MD FRS, who was married to John's daughter, and Anthony Benn, who was married to his grand-daughter, also served as Trustees.

Throughout his career John Spedding's devotion to the Lowther cause was complete. In modern parlance he would be described as a workaholic, but he demonstrated considerable business acumen. His accounts were kept meticulously, and he maintained a long and detailed correspondence with his employer. In addition to his own interests, he controlled the day-to-day affairs of Lowther's Whitehaven estate and, although major policy decisions were invariably referred to Sir James, he usually acted as adviser in those instances too. However, Spedding had a darker side to his character. That he was ruthless, deceitful, and at times dishonest cannot be denied. He even advised Sir James of a method to cheat the Customs at Whitehaven. For probably 30 years he was the most powerful man in Whitehaven and as such made many enemies. Other merchants, particularly Walter Lutwidge, complained bitterly of their inability to gain access to Lowther, But Sir James ruled that Spedding be a party to all his business.

John lived for many years at 141/2 Queen Street, where he died. The house was later occupied by William Brownrigg, who had married his daughter Mary.

Carlisle Spedding, 1695-1755

Carlisle was 10 years younger than his brother John and he joined the Lowther service in 1710, after plans to send him to sea had failed. At the time, John was colliery steward, and Carlisle began work as his assistant. He learned quickly and, particularly after his own appointment as colliery steward in 1730, gained a national reputation and was recognised as one of the leading mining engineers of the 18th century. He was responsible for the sinking of many new pits in the area and the enlarging of others. He is probably best known for the sinking of Saltom Pit, regarded by many at the time as the finest example of mining engineering and technology.

At one stage in his career, Carlisle considered leaving the colliery. Dissatisfied with his salary of £30 per year, which would 'but just get his Family bread and that with the utmost Frugality', he seriously considered leaving to take charge of a Newcomen engine elsewhere. He was persuaded to stay by his brother John, who increased his salary to £35.

Carlisle also gained a reputation as an architect. The finest example of his work is St James church which he designed and built in 1752/3. His son Thomas was appointed by Lowther as the first incumbent.

The younger Spedding was first nominated to the Board of Trustees by Sir James in 1718, at the age of only twenty-three. Remarkably he was also nominated as Lowther's deputy at meetings which Sir James could not attend. He remained a nominated Trustee until 1752, when, no doubt to facilitate Sir James's restructuring of the Board at the time of the dismissal of Walter Lutwidge, Carlisle became an 'elected' Trustee, which he remained until his death in 1755.

Carlisle Spedding was preoccupied throughout his career with the development of the Lowther mining enterprise. His achievements both in terms of coal output and technical innovation were remarkable. His involvement in the affairs of the town and Harbour was not great, but he, like John, naturally took the view that Harbour developments should favour the coal interest. In 1748 at the time of the debate as to whether another harbour should be built, he commented that 'the number of Colliers belonging to the Town more than the Harbour will contain in safety is 60. The Building of an outer Harbour would cost several Thousand pounds more than our duties upon the present Act would raise'.

In the early 1750s, Carlisle built the Whingill waggonway, and had begun work on Bransty Arch, when he was killed in a pit explosion on 8 August 1755. He was succeeded as colliery steward by his son James, who also became principal estate steward on the death of his uncle John in 1758.

Carlisle lived at 109 Scotch Street from 1718, where his widow was still living in 1762. He also owned 17 Irish Street which was occupied by his son Thomas from 1762 to 1780. Among his architectural achievements may have been the house at 30 Roper Street, built by his nephew James in 1745. Both John and Carlisle were careful to name their sons after Sir James Lowther. Each had a son named James, and John named his second son Lowther.

There was a close connection between the families of John Spedding and Peter How, an alliance which was important at the height of the tobacco trade. Spedding's son Lowther first married in 1739 Jane Walker, step-daughter of Peter How. Lowther's second wife (1741) was Christian Crakeplace who, after Lowther's death, married Peter How. John Spedding's cousin was Anthony Bacon, who for some time was trained in the Whitehaven estate office to become successor to Spedding. Bacon, however, chose to go to sea as a captain in the Maryland tobacco trade and subsequently settled in London as a merchant. In 1752, John Spedding persuaded Peter How, Richard Kelswick and other Whitehaven tobacco merchants to make him their agent. Bacon grew extremely prosperous, and eventually became an M.P. and a major figure in the coal and iron industries of Cumberland.

Sir James had complete trust in the Speddings and employed them fully in the management of his affairs. He recognised how much he owed them by rewarding them handsomely in his will: John received £1,000 and Carlisle £500. The Speddings, on their side, gave many years of devoted service and played an important part in the successes gained at Whitehaven during the 18th century.

Sources

The Minute Books of the Board of Trustees of the Town and Harbour of Whitehaven, 1708-1802.

The Acts of Parliament:

    1708 - 7 Anne.
    1711 - 10 Anne.
    1739 - 13 Geo 2.
    1760 - 1 Geo 3.
    1761 - 2 Geo 3.
    1787 - 28 Geo 3.

Local newspapers, especially the *Cumberland Pacquet*.

Whitehaven Town Book 1706-1782.

Becket, J.V., *Coal and Tobacco* (1981).

Collier, Sylvia, and Pearson, Sarah, *Whitehaven 1660-1800* (1991).

Dixon, Joshua MD, *The literary life of William Brownrigg to which are added an Account of the Coal Mines near Whitehaven and Observations on the Means of Preventing Epidemic Fevers* (1801).

Hay, D., *An Illustrated History of Whitehaven* (1979).

Fletcher, Isaac, MP FRS, *The Archaeology of the West Cumberland Coal Trade* (1877).

Lewis, M.J.T., *Early Wooden Railways*.

Morison, S.E., *John Paul Jones, A Sailor's Biography* (1959).

Owen, C.H.H., *The Lowther Family* (1990).

Parson, William, and White, William, *History, Gazetteer and Directory of the Counties of Cumberland and Westmorland* (1829).

Prevost, W.A.J., *A Trip to Whitehaven to Visit the Coal Works there in 1739 by Sir John Clerke* (1739).

Prior, J.M., *France and the Chesapeake*, 2 vols. (1973).

Spedding, John, A Notebook found in Somerset House in the Nineteenth Century.

Wood, O., *West Cumberland Coal 1600-1982/3* (1988).

Part Two

The 19th Century

Chapter 8

The Development of the Harbour 1802-22

Background

At the beginning of the 19th century, Whitehaven was still a port of major national economic significance. It was considered to be one of the first half dozen ports of the kingdom, having some 200 vessels with a total of 30,000 tons. Large quantities of coal were exported, and rum from the West Indies, and timber from America and the Baltic region were among the commodities imported.

At this period the Harbour consisted of the New Pier and the Old Pier on the west side, and on the east side the North Wall, which ran out from the shore for a distance of about 250 yards north west and then turned to the west for about 100 yards. The interior of the Harbour consisted of four basins, divided from each other by the Old Tongue, the New Tongue, and the Bulwark. The total area of the Harbour was about 32 acres. Owing to the large volume of trade, the accommodation had become insufficient and the exposed situation of the Harbour was a great drawback. Indeed, the Trustees even considered the purchase of an old ship to be sunk near the Harbour entrance 'to still the Old Harbour'.

17   St Nicholas' church and Queen Street in 1800. This is the church built in 1693.

79

The first Earl of Lonsdale (Wicked Jimmy) died in 1802 at the age of 66 years. On 24 May his Whitehaven estates were inherited by his 44-year-old distant cousin Sir William Lowther of Swillington (near Leeds), who became the 2nd Viscount Lowther of Whitehaven, and in 1807 the earldom of Lonsdale was re-established in his favour. Sir William's first task was to sort out the old earl's affairs and, in doing so, to try to restore the family's reputation. Lord Lonsdale left a great many debts, the most notorious of which was the £5,000 owing to the Wordsworth family for some 20 years. Sir William repaid the debt which, with accrued interest, totalled £8,500.

A general election was due in a few weeks, and Lord Lonsdale had intended to make yet another attempt to gain control of the two Carlisle seats. He had already made several unsuccessful attempts, all of which had resulted in elections accompanied by serious rioting, but he had set aside 9,000 guineas for another bitter struggle. Sir William, however, simply proposed that the Blue and Yellow parties should each nominate a member, thereby avoiding the inevitable expense and violence of a contested election.

The Trustees of the Town and Harbour found the old earl difficult to deal with, and may well have anticipated similar problems with the incoming viscount. The Harbour was sorely in need of repair and further development, and there is no doubt that the Trustees looked to Lord Lowther for a lead. He seems to have been most amenable and helpful; nevertheless, the Trustees, in a gesture of appeasement, frequently recorded in their minutes, 'That whatever Plan or Plans Lord Lowther conceived to be expedient for the Improvement and Safety of the Harbour, it is the wish of the Trustees to concur fully therein'. Lord Lowther thus restored the relationship between himself and the Trustees; he held and wielded the power, and he took the initiative in the development of the Harbour.

The Creation of North Harbour

The Trustees invited Captain Huddart of Allonby, a noted hydrographer, to make recommendations for extensions to the Harbour, with particular emphasis on the need to create an area between the Bulwark and the North Wall which would provide a calm harbour in times of bad weather, and reduce the swirling action of the sea which disturbed the inner Harbour.

Captain Huddart's solution of the problem consisted of: the addition of a splay to the Old Pier, the remodelling and the addition of an acutely angled splay to the North Wall, and the repositioning and widening of the Bulwark. The two splays created an entrance to the inner Harbour 50 yards wide. The Bulwark, which had previously pointed towards the Old Pier, was taken down and rebuilt several degrees towards the north, the seaward end being moved until it pointed towards the new splay on the North Wall. This created a new North Harbour, with its entrance between the Bulwark and the North Wall splay, but on the inner side of, and at right angles to, the entrance to the inner Harbour created by the Old Pier and the North Wall. Work began in 1804 and continued at an expenditure of some £4,000 per year until 1809. Although the new Harbour created additional space for the mooring of ships, the problem of the vulnerability of the shipping in bad weather, particularly from the west and north west, was not completely solved.

The Trustees at this time were in a sound financial position. In 1801, they had favourable cash balances of some £6,000 which, together with average annual incomes of £1,800 and modest bank borrowings, enabled them to pay for these major works without difficulty. Bank overdrafts reached a peak of £6,500 in 1809, but were cleared in the following five years as income increased and expenditure was reduced.

The Act of 1806

The Census Return for 1801 shows the population of Whitehaven as 8,742. To this figure must be added the number of people living in the immediately adjoining areas of Corkickle, Ginns, New Houses and Mount Pleasant: the total population therefore might have reached 12,000.

The town was beset by a series of social problems which included poverty, disease, and food shortages. The sanitary state of the town was appalling; there was no water supply, and the building regulations so carefully laid down by Sir John Lowther in the late 17th century were no longer strictly applied.

Crime and disorder were also serious problems in the town—burglary and breaking and entering were particularly common offences. There were also several riots, protests and demonstrations: the seamen, the most numerous group, were ever prone to riot, either on account of the activities of the press gangs, or their many quarrels with the ships' masters over pay. The coal miners and shipyard workers were also involved in many incidents of disorderly behaviour for similar reasons. The Riot Act was read on more than one occasion in Whitehaven during the 18th century, and disturbances were often quelled by the intervention of troops garrisoned at Carlisle—the only assistance available to the magistrates at the time.

Sir William, keen to try to solve these problems, obtained an Act of Parliament (46 Geo 3 Cap 115), 'for continuing and amending several Acts of Parliament for improving the Port, Harbour, and Town of Whitehaven ...'. This Act, basically a town improvement Act, provided for the 'Paving of the Streets, the Flagging of Pavements, the setting up of a Fire Service, the fixing of Gutters and Downspouts to the buildings, the appointment of Watchmen, the Licensing of Carriers Carts, and other regulations for the general improvement of the Town'. There was even a requirement that each householder should sweep and clean the frontage of his or her house every Monday, Wednesday and Saturday, between 8 and 10 a.m., with a fine of 10s. for failure to do so! Powers were provided to levy rates on property to cover the costs of improvements.

Also in this Act were provisions for amending the harbour duties. In addition to the existing tonnage duties, all ships entering the Harbour were to pay a further 1d. per ton. The Trustees were given powers to increase or decrease the rates of duties and charges which had remained virtually unchanged since 1709. After a reduction of the rates, the Trustees were allowed to increase them again, but not above the level laid down in the Acts. There was the further stipulation that rates could not be reduced without the approval of the bondholders holding five-eighths of the amount remaining unpaid.

The tonnage of ships was to be ascertained from the Ship's Register (established in 1786) and the ship's master was required to produce the Certificate of Registry. In the event of a dispute, the following formula was provided for the calculation of the tonnage of a ship:

Drop a Plumb Line over the Stem of the ship. Measure the distance between the Plumb Line and the after part of the Stern Post at the level of the Load Water Mark. From this, deduct the measurement from the top of the Plumb Line, taken parallel to the water, to a point perpendicularly over the Load Water Mark at the Fore Part of the Main Stem. From the result, further deduct 3" in every foot for the rake abaft, and also three fifths of the ships breadth for the rake forward. The remainder equals the Just Length of the Keel. The Breadth of the Ship shall be taken from the outside of the Plank in the broadest part of the ship, above or below the Main Wales, excluding sheathing and doubling. The Tonnage of the ship is then to be found by multiplying the Just Length of the Keel by the Breadth of the Ship, and that product by Half the Breadth, and by dividing the result by ninety four.

Anyone found guilty of obstructing the persons making the measurements was liable to a fine of £5! The Act also provided that wilful damage to the piers and the deliberate extinguishing of the lights set up in the Harbour were offences to be classified as felonies. The penalty for either, on conviction, was seven years' transportation.

The Harbour, after the work carried out during the period 1804-9, was acknowledged to be considerably improved, but the ship owners were constantly agitating for better protection from the weather. The Trustees, in 1812, recorded that they were of the opinion 'that the Harbour is, in its present state, insecure, and that an Exterior Guard is wanting to protect the Interior part of the Harbour'. At the same time representatives of the ship owners addressed a petition to Lord Lonsdale requesting some improvement of the Harbour.

The Trustees consulted many eminent engineers from time to time, but the best schemes came from Mr. John Rennie. In 1814, Rennie proposed two schemes: (a) To extend the New Pier nearly north east for 250 yards, and the North Wall for 140 yards, thus making an entrance 60 yards wide. A hundred feet within each head, he proposed to build a jetty 100ft. long at right angles to the piers. These would not only check the inrun of the sea, but also would protect the piers themselves; (b) He proposed to build a pier having three cants. The first was to commence at about the centre of the New Pier, and taking a direction north north east for 110 yards, the second north east by east for the same distance, and the third nearly north east for a similar distance, making a total length of 330 yards. The North Wall was to be extended by 60 yards, and jetties were to be provided similar to those in scheme (a). The estimate for scheme (a) amounted to £96,115, and for (b) £119,176, a difference of £23,061. Rennie strongly recommended scheme (b) as, in his opinion, it was much the better scheme.

In March 1814, Rennie wrote to say that he had sent 'on the Glasgow Mail Coach, a Tin Case containing Mr Peile's Surveys and my Plans for the Improvements'. However, it was not until November 1815 that the Trustees formally accepted the plans, and then for the construction of a west pier only. On Mr. Rennie's recommendation, the Trustees shortly afterwards appointed John Young, then assistant engineer at Leith Docks, as supervisor of the works at a salary of £200 per annum.

The new works were of very considerable extent, and consequently a great deal of preparatory work was necessary. In order to provide the huge quantity of stones required, it was deemed advisable to use two quarries, one on either side of the Harbour. The one at Bransty was to be connected by railway to the head of the North Wall, using for a large part of the distance the existing William Pit waggonway. This project required the construction of a wall six yards high and 500 yards long, and an additional 600 yards of railway. A crane was to be placed at the head of the North Wall where the stones were to be lowered into specially constructed boats to be taken across the Harbour to the new pier for use on the new west pier. The total cost of this part of the scheme was estimated at £850.

A new quarry was to be opened on the south side of the Harbour at Whaite Field, some distance from the bowling green. An inclined plane was to be built on arches from the new pier to the bowling green, and a double track railway built to a length of about five hundred yards. The cost of this part of the scheme was expected to be £750. Lord Lonsdale showed considerable interest in this work, and offered the full use of the colliery railways and a supply of iron work at first cost. Both projects were to be under the immediate supervision of John Peile, Lonsdale's agent. On 14 November 1816, work was ordered to begin as soon as possible, 'under the present distressed state of the Labouring Classes and Want of Employment'. This was the period following the end of the Napoleonic Wars when the country was in the depths of severe recession.

Lord Lonsdale and the Trustees were well aware that the undertaking they had embarked on could not be paid for from existing funds and harbour duties. They therefore determined to obtain another Act of Parliament to enable them to increase the tonnage duties and to redraft the scale of charges on goods and merchandise.

The Act of 1816

Under the Act of 1816 (56 Geo III Cap 44) all former tonnage duties, rates and charges ceased on 29 September 1816 and were replaced by the following:

> Tonnage duties which were to apply to all ships except those in the service of the King, H.M. Customs, and the Post Master General
>
> Inwards:
> - from any Part of Great Britain, Ireland and the Isle of Man—6d per ton.
> - from any other Part of Europe, the Isles of Guernsey, Jersey, Alderney, Sark, the Faro Islands and Iceland—1/-per ton.
> - from any part of Asia, Africa or America to the Northward of the River La Plata inclusive, and to the Northward of the Cape of Good Hope, the Islands of St. Helena, Ascension, Cape de Verde Islands, Canaries, Western Islands, Madeira, Azores, Newfoundland, Greenland and Davies's Streights—1/6 per ton.
> - from any part of South America to the Southward of the Rio La Plata, in the Pacific Ocean, in Africa or Asia to the Eastward of the Cape of Good Hope —2/- per ton.
>
> Outwards:
> - to any Part of Great Britain, Ireland and the Isle of Man—exempt from Tonnage Duty.
> - to any other part of the World—6d per ton, but if in Ballast only, One Moiety thereof.

The new rates of duties payable on goods and merchandise were detailed in a schedule many pages long showing the type of goods and the amount payable. It contained many day-to-day items:

> Tobacco @ 1/8 per ton, Sugar @ 2/- per ton, Barley @ 4d per quarter etc.

Some odd items:

> Bugles @ 2/- per ton!, Feathers @ 6d per cwt, Elephants Teeth @ 6d per cwt

And some bizarre items:

> Argol @ 2/- per ton, Morels @ 4d per cwt, Succades @ 1d per cwt.

The new rates were payable in full on imports, and also at a quarter of the rate on exports to any part of Great Britain, Ireland and the Isle of Man, and at half rate if exported to any other part of the world. Whitehaven's principal export, coal, was charged at three halfpence per chaldron regardless of destination. There was also a change in the hopper duties, the new rate being 1s. per ton of ballast discharged.

By 1814, the average annual income of the Harbour had reached £4,500, and it was calculated that the new proposed rates would at least double that figure. The income for 1814 was as follows:

Tonnage Duties:
Vessels from G.B., Ireland and I.O.M.	2327	14	5
Foreign Vessels @ 5d and 9d per Ton	169	13	3
Duties on Merchandize Imported	624	11	6
Duty on Coal Exported @ 1d per Chaldron	486	3	0
Harbour Lighting @ 1d per Ton	158	19	10
Hopper Income @ 6d per Ton of Ballast	953	6	0
	£4720	8	0

Assuming that the new rates were in force, the income would have been £11,075.

Some of the penalties were also changed. Those found guilty of wilful damage to the piers, or of extinguishing the harbour lights, were no longer subject to seven years' transportation, but merely had to pay for any damage caused. For loosing or cutting ships' mooring ropes there was a fine of £50 plus the cost of any damage, while for leaving goods lying on the quays for more than 48 hours, there was a penalty of 5s. per hour.

Most importantly, the Trustees were empowered to borrow £130,000 by issuing Harbour Bonds on the security of future tonnage duties, merchandise rates, and hopper duties. In the event that this amount proved to be insufficient, or that exceptional repair costs were incurred as a result of storm damage to the works in progress, Lonsdale and 17 of the Trustees were enabled to borrow an additional £50,000. At the same time they were to increase the duties and rates by up to 25 per cent, and were not to reduce them until the £130,000 had been repaid.

The town improvement aspects of the 1816 Act were particularly important: The Trustees were required to focus their attention on such matters as the operation of a police force, street lighting, street cleaning, the macadamising of the roads, the numbering of the houses and so on. 'The Trustees shall and they are hereby authorized and required to cause the Streets, Lanes ... to be properly Paved, Watched, Lighted, and secured against Fire, and to supply the same with Water'. The water this time was to be brought from Adams Gill, Moresby Gill and Bransty Gill. The Trustees were also empowered to extend the area over which they had jurisdiction by incorporating streets and parts of the adjacent Preston Quarter, in the township of Whitehaven. These areas were not annexed but became part of the lamp and paving rate area of Whitehaven. The Act also provided that all 'Pavements, Flagstones, Fire Engines, Watch Boxes etc' became the property of the Trustees: a situation which was to be the cause of much controversy on the creation of the Borough of Whitehaven in the 1890s.

A great deal of work was carried out in the town as a result of this Act, and it was readily financed from rates income, including the formation of a police force but, unfortunately, still nothing was done about the water supply.

The New West Pier (1)

Work began on the preparatory facilities at the Harbour in late 1816 under the joint supervision of John Peile, Lowther's Agent, and of John Young, supervisor of the works reporting to John Rennie, and continued steadily until September 1817.

At this stage the Trustees were alarmed to find that the greatly increased tonnage duties were discouraging ship owners from using the Harbour and, coupled with the depressed state of trade, there was a substantial reduction in Harbour income. They were keen to reduce the duties but, after careful scrutiny, decided that, under the terms of the recently obtained Act of 1816, they were not able to do so. Lonsdale accused them of making much ado about very little and told them to reduce the duties on his responsibility. The Trustees agreed, but pressed Lord Lonsdale to obtain a further Act of Parliament to allow them specifically to increase or decrease the duties as they saw fit. Lonsdale was not pleased by this incident, but obtained the Act of 1818 (58 Geo III Cap 15) which permitted the Trustees to go ahead.

On 1 September 1817 they reduced all duties and rates by 25 per cent, except the tonnage duty on ships arriving from Great Britain, Ireland and the Isle of Man, which was reduced by 50 per cent. Most curiously, only one week later, on 8 September 1817, the Trustees announced that the reduced rates and the lack of trade had reduced income to a level which was insufficient to justify the continuation of the Harbour development. They ordered that works under construction should be secured against sea and weather, and then that all work should be suspended.

The arches for the inclined plane near the new pier were in an advanced state of construction, and needed only the building of parapet walls '3 feet high, finished with common square coping' and some rubble infill. On the Bransty Site, the breast wall needed to be completed 'to the height required for the railway', and the structure secured against the sea. John Young was instructed to complete the work as necessary, and to dismiss all workpeople not required. He was also given notice that his own contract would be terminated. Lord Lonsdale and Mr. Rennie were fully informed of these decisions. Young's departure was delayed as the Trustees required him to supervise repairs to the Half Moon Battery, which was severely damaged in a November gale. Young resigned on 25 January 1818, although his notice did not expire until 1 March.

The financial situation of the Trust was still very sound, the annual income being actually a little better than in 1814, and it was certainly not falling. The bank accounts were in credit, and no use had been made of the Trustees' borrowing powers of

£130,000. The actions of the Trustees at this time seem to be at least a little strange and over hasty. Could it be that with the preparatory work nearing completion, the whole scheme was abandoned because the Trustees no longer favoured the design of the new pier?

The Accounts for the 12 months to 25 March 1819 read:

COLLECTORS ACCOUNTS
INCOMES

Amount of Harbour Tonnage	2525	2	11
Lamp Tonnage	309	9	10
Ballast	847	13	6
Duty on Goods Imported	969	12	6
Duty on Goods Exported	770	13	7
Use of Quay Hawser	23	2	0
Use of Ballast Tubs		8	0
Profits of Harbour Boat	37	9	0
Penalties and Fines	25	0	0
Rents Receivable	4	4	0
Income from Baths	53	10	0
	£5566	5	4

EXPENDITURE

Old Harbour	1997	2	9
New Harbour	1440	8	1
Balance paid to Treasurer	2128	14	6
	£5566	5	4

TREASURERS ACCOUNTS

Cash Balances Brought Forward				6653	9	4
Interest Received on Exchequer Bills				75	11	8
Interest Received on Bank Deposits				104	9	9
Balance Received from Collector				2128	14	6
				£8962	5	3
Costs re Purchase of Exchequer Bills				44	18	8
Amount invested in Exchequer Bills				8000	0	0
Bank Balances - Hartley	411	12	6			
- Johnston, Raney	505	14	1			
				917	6	7
				£8962	5	3

When this financial situation is compared with that in 1814, the Trustees could hardly plead poverty as the reason for abandoning work on the new pier.

It was not until three years later that the Trustees took any further action regarding the state of the Harbour. In February 1821 they called for a report on the condition of all the quays and piers, which revealed that there had been some neglect and that major repair work was needed as a matter of urgency (see chapter 12). The Trustees gave orders for work to begin immediately on the lighthouse, the Harbour Master's office and the straightening of the Bulwark. They also began again to quarry for stones. This began a period during which the relationship between Lord Lonsdale and the Trustees became increasingly strained. A series of actions by the Trustees only irritated his lordship, whose sole aim was to see work recommence on the new west pier. He simply could not understand why the Trustees apparently wished only to tinker with the existing harbour, and seemed indifferent to the larger scheme. In June 1821, Lonsdale wrote that he could not approve the quarrying of stones, as 'he could not understand why it was necessary as the Trustees had no specific use for them'. At their next meeting the Trustees resolved to continue the quarrying of stones.

The Trustees debated the relative merits of Patent Slips and dry docks for use in repairing ships out of the water. In opting for slips, three Trustees were delegated to travel to Leith to see Mr. Morton, inventor of the Patent Slip, and to see the machine in action. The three Trustees eventually reported that the slip was an ingenious piece of equipment, and that one was vital for Whitehaven. Lonsdale was furious when he discovered that the Trustees in question had not even been to Leith.

Lonsdale contacted the Admiralty for their opinion of the Morton slip, and on receiving a favourable reply, ordered one for Whitehaven. He also informed the Trustees that he would buy it, choose the site for it, and would also operate it. The Trustees, in their turn, argued that the slip should be part of the Harbour facilities controlled by them, and chose a site, which incidentally, was on land owned by Lonsdale and then employed for other purposes. On 22 May 1822 Lonsdale ordered the slip and sited it near East Strand. It was 400 feet long, capable of accommodating three vessels of 300 tons burthen, and could haul up a ship of 450 tons. The slip cost £1,675, and was built in three months; when it came into operation, it was operated on behalf of Lord Lonsdale.

The Trustees next ordered that 'the Slip on the New Quay be repaired and made more commodious and safe for persons going into and landing from Boats, and that a rail or chain be placed at the end of the Quay as may be deemed necessary to secure persons from falling into the sea'. They also ordered that the timber slip into the Old Harbour should be repaired and enlarged at a cost of £144. Further, they also resolved that 300 copies of the income and expenditure account should be printed for distribution to ship owners and others paying duties.

Evidently, Lord Lonsdale lost patience with the Trustees. He responded with the following letter, addressed to Richard Blakeney, Secretary to the Trustees:

4 September 1822

I have received your letter of the 2nd inst enclosing the Minutes of the proceedings at a Meeting of the Trustees of the Harbour of Whitehaven on that day.

It has not been usual since I was connected with the Town of Whitehaven for the Trustees to Sanction the Erection of any new Works or to provide for the Extension of old ones, except in case of particular necessity or of some obvious advantage likely to result from it. No such ground appears to be laid for the proposition respecting the Timber Slip. Under the peculiar circumstances in which we are placed at this moment, I had hoped the Trustees would have seen the necessity of adhering to the old principals, and that any project of this kind might at least have been delayed till after it should be seen whether the visit of Messrs Rennie and Whidby on the questions to be submitted to them on the 3rd of next month, may induce the Trustees to undertake the work so long in contemplation.

With respect to the publication of the Account, I have to say that no reason is stated, and none presents itself to my mind to induce me to think that the practice which has prevailed since the Establishment of the Harbour should now be departed from.

I am Sir etc   Lonsdale.

At their meeting on 7 October 1822, at which Lord Lonsdale was present, the Trustees resolved that 'the Alteration to the Timber Slip as recommended on 2 September be adopted' and that 'the Accounts be printed and published as decided on 2 September'. However, Lord Lonsdale had prevailed upon the Trustees to invite Sir John Rennie, son of the John Rennie whose advice had been sought in 1814, together with Mr. Whidby, to visit Whitehaven and make recommendations for further developments. They produced a plan which the Trustees resolved 'be immediately adopted'.

The character of the Board remained virtually unchanged throughout the early 19th century. Traders, manufacturers, wines and spirits merchants, rope makers, bankers, solicitors, doctors and clergymen were all represented on the Board over the years. Among the most prominent were the Jeffersons (wines and spirit merchants), the Hartleys (rope makers and bankers), William Miller (tannery owner), William Younghusband (ship owner and merchant), and Rev. Henry Lowther (clergyman).

The leading figure, however, was John Peile, Lord Lonsdale's principal agent. Arguably, Peile was the most able man ever produced by Whitehaven, and for a period of almost 50 years was one of the town's most eminent citizens. From 1811 until 1848 he duplicated the role of John Spedding a century previously. Within a few years of his appointment, the coal mines, as a result of his work, were described as the most up-to-date in the country. He was responsible for the supervision of much of the work on the Harbour, and for many of the buildings in the town.

As was the case with Spedding, Peile's influence with Lonsdale, and his involvement in the affairs of the town and Harbour, made him many enemies, but there can be no doubt that this work was of the greatest benefit to Lonsdale's interests and to Whitehaven generally.

Chapter 9

Harbour Development 1824-58

The Proposed Act of Parliament, 1824

There was a proposition, in 1792, to build a new sea wall between the existing North Wall and Redness Point. The land on which it was to be built was outside the harbour limits, and Lord Lonsdale and the Trustees could not agree on the exact boundaries of the land required. The Act of 1792 incorporated the land within the harbour limits, but noted that the exact area was in dispute, and that the matter was to go to arbitration. On 13 November 1792, the arbiters, Sir Joseph Senhouse of Arkleby Hall for the Trustees, and George Vickers of Whitehaven for Lord Lonsdale, made the following award:

> The ground to be made use of for enlarging the said Harbour extends from a place called Redness Point Eastward of the said Harbour on the Outside of a Wall intended to be erected until it reaches within 120 yards of the present outward Works of the Pier or Quay of the present Harbour and from thence in a Line until it comes within 40 yards of what was called the Old Pier or Quay on the 1st January last, and from thence to the North Side of the Sugar House Bulwark. From thence along the Sugar House Bulwark, along the Sea Shore until it meets the aforesaid Redness Point, and that the said ground is and shall be the right of the said James Earl of Lonsdale his Heirs and Assigns, and that the other part of the Ground now made use of for the present Harbour is and shall be the right of the Trustees of the said Harbour agreeable to the powers vested in them by Act of Parliament.

This award made the piece of land virtually a separate harbour, although it was included within the harbour limits, over which, it must be stressed, the Trustees had no powers. In the event, the proposed wall was not built, and indeed no developments took place in this part of the Harbour before 1824, when it was considered that the proposed new North Wall might well be built there.

Consequently, Lord Lonsdale undertook to transfer to the Trustees the land over which he held the rights. As this required an Act of Parliament, Lonsdale instructed his solicitor, Hodgson, to draft an appropriate Bill, and submit it to the Trustees. The

Trustees, for their part, appointed Wilson Perry, a Whitehaven attorney, to peruse and report on the draft Bill.

Perry reported that not only did the Bill incorporate the Harbour land, but that all the preceding Acts had been virtually rewritten, and he listed the following objections:

(1) The Draft referred to 'The Town and Harbour of Whitehaven in the Manor of St Bees'. This was the first time that this had been done in the several Acts, and because Lonsdale was Lord of the Manor of St Bees, the question arose as to whether his rights to hold Courts Leet and Baron would interfere with the authority of the Trustees in respect of Whitehaven.

(2) The Draft gave powers to the Trustees for '21 years' and not 'for ever' as in preceding Acts. Therefore it was held, the powers of the Trustees could cease at the end of that period and revert to Lonsdale.

(3) It was held that the powers of the Trustees would be curtailed in that the approval of Lonsdale had to be sought for almost every action. There were to be three classifications of powers: (a) by the Trustees alone, (b) requiring the concurrence of Lonsdale, and (c) requiring the presence of Lonsdale. It was clear that powers in the first category were to be greatly reduced.

(4) Meetings of Trustees not called by Lonsdale were to be held null and void. This provision alone, it was held, would give him total power.

(5) The draft contained a provision to increase the rates on the town to help to pay for the harbour extensions. This would exacerbate the 'Town v Harbour' situation, as there were already many complaints about the burden of the rates.

(6) The Bill proposed to include ratepayers as voters at the elections of Trustees. However, as they were not to be allowed to vote for Harbour Trustees, did this mean that there were to be separate Town Trustees?

(7) The franchise was to be altered to exclude 'Masters of Vessels'. Perry made no comment on this, but proposed that the Trustees should require that a more precise attempt be made to define 'Those dealing by way of Goods and Merchandise ...'. He advised that the vote be restricted to exporters and importers only and also that voters should be resident in Whitehaven.

(8) Provision was made for the merging of the town and Harbour accounts, which had been kept separate as required by the Act of 1708. This, it was thought, would facilitate the use of 'Town' monies for 'Harbour' purposes and vice versa, a situation considered to be most improper.

(9) The offices of clerk and treasurer (collector) to the Board of Trustees were to be merged; again a suggestion thought to be most irregular.

(10) All town improvements were to be subject to approval by Lord Lonsdale. The Trustees objected strongly to interference, as they saw it, by his lordship in the affairs of the town.

(11) Lonsdale reserved the right to build railways and other structures on the moles and piers without reference to the Trustees.

The Trustees were disturbed by the extent of the changes proposed, and accused Lord Lonsdale of trying to extend and increase his powers over the town and Harbour at the expense of theirs. They also insisted that they should have a representative in attendance, in addition to Lonsdale's solicitor, at any future work to be done on the Bill. They voted therefore to reject the draft Bill.

Lonsdale wrote to the Trustees in January 1825 expressing dismay that the Trustees should think that he was 'seeking by indirect means the opportunity of extending the privileges granted under the former Acts to the Lord of the Manor. Disclaiming yet again as I do in the most positive manner any intention or even the remotest wish to act on the principle imputed to me ...'.

In view of the contents of this letter, it is difficult to understand what Lord Lonsdale was trying to do. Although the tone of Perry's comments indicates suspicion of Lonsdale's motives, the proposed changes really were fundamental to the operation of the Board of Trustees, a body which had been in existence for over 100 years.

Work continued on the draft Bill, with Wilson Perry acting as the Trustees' legal representative, until September 1826, when it was resubmitted to the Trustees for their examination. (Perry was elected to the Board of Trustees in August of that year.) This time a committee had been formed to study the Bill—John Brocklebank Jnr, Isaac Littledale, Milham Hartley, William Miller, Richard Barker and Wilson Perry.

The committee was very surprised to find that the new draft was almost exactly the same as the one rejected in 1824, and that the Trustees' input over the intervening period had been virtually ignored. In fact the Trustees, if anything, were to have their powers even more restricted. For instance, they were not to have control over the monies in their hands, as transactions could not be carried out without Lord Lonsdale's agreement. Again the Act was to have force for '21 years' only instead of 'forever'; a point to which the Trustees took the greatest exception.

On reporting back, the committee, recommending rejection of the Bill, commented, 'it would be the Duty of the Trustees to oppose such a Measure by every Means in their Power, as it would certainly be the Extreme of Folly to consent to the Repeal of Acts perpetual in their Duration, and receive in Return an Act of a few years continuance only'.

The priorities of the Trustees at this time, however, lay with the harbour developments and they were anxious to know whether they would be acting legally over the positioning of the projected North Pier, and also whether it would be legal for them to charge Harbour duties on the new piers.

Counsel's opinion was sought, therefore, which confirmed that, as the new piers were extensions of existing piers, they did not require any beach land, and therefore did not interfere with anyone's property. Similarly, the pier extensions would attract Harbour duties in the same way as did the piers from which the extensions were made. Further, the Trustees were informed that the Lord of the Manor could not rescind a legal resolution of the Board, and also that the Lord of the Manor could not retrospectively withdraw his consent to a course of action.

Armed with this information, on 3 March 1827 the Trustees formally rejected the draft Bill, and instructed their solicitor to proceed no further with the matter.

The New West Pier (2)

At the end of 1822 the Trustees invited Sir John Rennie and Mr. Whidby to submit their plans. They proposed a pier running north-north-west from the western corner of the New Quay for 145 yards, then canting north east for 110 yards, and again canting east north east for a similar distance. The pier was designed to provide as much water as possible at low water (minimum 8 feet 6 inches) at the pier head, and to make the water smooth within it, 'so that ships may enter with ease and safety within the Pier at an early part of the tide'. The estimated cost of the new pier was £67,274 18s. 0d.; it will be noticed that although similar, this was not the plan which had been adopted in 1815/6.

The plans were presented for formal acceptance on 16 June 1823, but John Brocklebank Jnr moved an amendment 'that the plan will so far exceed the means at the disposal of the Trustees, that it would be highly injurious to the best interests of the Town to attempt carrying it into effect'. The amendment was lost, six votes for, 13 against, and the plans were approved 11 votes to eight. As can be seen, the plans for the new pier were by no means approved unanimously! At the same meeting it was reported that the funds of the Trust amounted to £19,200-£16,000 in Exchequer bills and £3,200 in balances at the local banks. It happened that 1823 was a Trustee election year and, after being re-elected, Brocklebank insisted that his amendment should be voted on again. This time he was defeated 14 to one, and consequently he resigned. (He was re-elected in 1826.)

Work recommenced almost immediately on the preliminary work for the new pier. John Peile was instructed to provide Sir John Rennie with:

A daily journal of the tides.

A set of soundings from the Harbour mouth half a mile out to sea.

A set of borings in the line of the proposed new pier to 15 or 20 feet below the sea bed.

The directions and velocities of the currents.

A section taken from the lower end of Lowther Street across the New Tongue and the Old Quay, showing the high and low water marks of spring tides.

A sketch of the coast from St Bees Head to Redness Point.

Peile was also instructed to 'finish the Iron Railway through William Pit Yard to the Quarries, and then to let the Trustees use it'. He was also required to complete the inclined plane to the New Quay, and to open the quarry at Whaite Field.

Sir John Rennie was appointed engineer in charge at a salary of £200 per annum, plus travelling and living expenses while at Whitehaven. At the same time John Fox was appointed as Sir John's resident assistant at a salary of £300 per annum, inclusive of house rent and all other costs.

Rennie presented a list of immediate requirements before work on the pier could commence. This included 40-50 tons of Pozzolana (a type of porous volcanic ash used in making hydraulic cements), a cargo of Aberthan lime, and the construction of a lime kiln and a horse-driven mortar mill, both to be sited as near the work as possible. The list also included a diving bell (which cost £1,038 1s. 5d.) to be used when setting stones under water, purpose-built boats to carry stones from the North Wall to the New Quay, and various cranes, waggons etc.

The lime kiln and mortar mill were built adjoining the Old Fort which was partially demolished and the stones were used in the erection of the kiln. William Bowes, the Whitehaven shipbuilder, constructed a shallow draft boat capable of carrying 20 tons of stones for £320. Contracts were entered into with local masons for the quarrying

TO MASONS.

WANTED at the Works at WHITEHAVEN HARBOUR, some good MASONS, qualified to dress and set large Stones, in Piers, or Works of a similar Nature.

Ten or Twelve Men who can be well recommended will meet with Encouragement and Employment, at the new Pier of Whitehaven Harbour : and have an Opportunity of being employed at Piece Work.

Application may be made to Mr. WHITE-SIDE, Clerk of the Trustees of Whitehaven Harbour, or to Mr. JOHN FOX. Superintendent of the said New Pier. Whitehaven, 26 April, 1824.   (17)

TO VISITORS.
JUST PUBLISHED,

18   Masons wanted to work on new West Pier, 1824.

and dressing of large quantities of stone, and 60 tons of iron rails were purchased from Dowlais Iron Co., Cardiff, at £5 10s. 0d. per ton, for the extensions to the various railways.

Work quickly got under way and proceeded without difficulties, so that on 21 May 1824 it was resolved 'that The Trustees proceed in a body to witness the Laying of the Foundation Stone of the new West Pier this evening at 6 o'clock, and that Mr John Peile be requested to lay the Foundation Stone in such direction as he thinks proper and best calculated to meet the projected improvement'. Ten barrels of beer were provided for the workpeople and others attending, and it was arranged for a salute by the guns to be fired in the Fort and the Half Moon Battery.

The Harbour work was carried on only during the summer months, and Sir John Rennie reported on progress to the Trustees each October. The new pier was expected to be built at a rate of about 30 yards each year. In 1824, 33 yards were achieved, in 1825—26 yards, in 1826—57 yards and in 1827—58 yards, a total of 174 yards in the first four years. At the end of that period, it was reported that 'its effect in tranquillizing the old entrance to the Harbour begins to be sensibly felt'.

Everything did not always go smoothly, of course. Rennie complained frequently that the supply of stones from the quarries was not keeping pace with the work on the pier, and also that he had to employ additional masons on site because many of the stones were inaccurately dressed. He did not like Mr. Bowes' boat, as he thought it was neither big enough nor robust enough. However, the diving bell was a great success: so much so that a second one was ordered.

On 14 August 1825, a bad storm severely damaged the new work. The contractor, Kenneth Mathieson, was held to be at fault in not having adhered to the specification and method of building. Mathieson abandoned the contract two days later, and the damaged work had to rebuilt.

At the end of the 1827 season, Rennie reported that the new pier had been completed '174 running yards', but the amount of cash available to the Trustees had fallen to £4,389. It was decided therefore to make use of the borrowing powers obtained in the Act of 1816, and advertisements were placed for £5,000 of Harbour Bonds in minimum amounts of £200.

The first applicants were:

Wilfred Lawson	2000	0	0
Isaac Littledale	500	0	0
William Richardson	500	0	0
The Trustees of Bootle School	416	11	0
	£3416	11	0

It was at this stage that Lord Lonsdale, infuriated by the Trustees' rejection of his draft Bill, gave them notice to quit his quarries. Deprived of a source of stones the

Trustees then decided to abandon the work and to build a head at the point reached. They instructed Mr. Fox to discontinue the acquisition of stones, and to dismiss all the workmen not required to complete the final stages. As a result, 130 men were dismissed. However, in November, they countermanded Fox's instructions about the stones, and advertisements were placed for money in order that work on the pier could be continued. On being informed of these decisions, Lonsdale wrote that, in view of the continued obstruction by the Trustees of the new Bill, he had no option but to withdraw his consent for further work to be carried out during 1828.

The Trustees, having taken legal advice, replied that they considered that the existing Acts of Parliament gave them all the powers they needed, and that a new Act would be superfluous. In any case, they contended that the Lord of the Manor could not rescind a legal resolution of the Trustees, and therefore could not withdraw his consent retrospectively, thereby wasting some £40,000. Lonsdale relented and withdrew the notice, but three months were lost before work resumed.

A great deal of progress was made in the 1828 season, and Rennie reported that the pier was now 245 yards long, 71 yards having been completed in the year. The diving bells had been used extensively as the end of the pier even at low water was still 11 feet below the surface. A violent gale from SW and WSW on 9 December forced out of position 50 to 60 yards of the parapet by some 18 inches, and the remedial work incorporated slight modifications in order to strengthen the structure.

Rennie, in October 1829, reported that the pier had reached a length of 306 yards—49 yards past the second cant: 'The effect of the New Pier in tranquillizing the Old Harbour, and in facilitating the entrance and departure of vessels to and from the sea at all times is, I am happy to observe, very satisfactory'. The Trustees voted to continue the work during 1830, but Mr. J. Brocklebank Jnr objected and presented an amendment that work on the pier should cease, that the harbour duties be reduced by 25 per cent, that the existing debts be paid off at £1,000 per year, and that funds be applied to repairs in the Old Harbour. The amendment was defeated by 12 votes to three.

The continuing extension of the pier was financed from Harbour income of some £6,500 per annum and by the borrowing against Harbour Bonds of a little over £27,000. During the three years ending March 1830, the Trustees had spent on the Harbour a total of £48,127, and viewed the future with sufficient confidence to turn away offers of loans of money—'the Trustees have engaged a sufficient sum for the present occasion of the Harbour'.

After consulting with Sir John Rennie, the Trustees decided that work on the new pier should be brought to a close at the end of the 1830 season, and John Fox was instructed to 'make a permanent head at the end of the seasons work, bearing in mind the erection of a lighthouse'. A simple square end was made to the pier which at the time was 359 yards in length, with the head in 15 feet of water at low tide. They also ordered the construction of a wall and surface paving between the new quay and the new pier 'to afford a better communication'. Lord Lonsdale immediately objected that the permission of the Lord of the Manor was necessary before either of these schemes could be started, adding that 'the erection of the Lighthouse is premature as the New Pier is not yet completed'.

The Trustees retorted that his lordship had given his consent on 23 June 1823 when he, along with a majority of the Trustees, had accepted Rennie's plans for the new pier. Lonsdale was still annoyed over the rejection of the proposed new Act of Parliament and, in continuing to withhold his approval of the building of the light-house, wrote to the Secretary—'I have to request that you will assure the Trustees that not one of them can regret more than I do the want of that confidence and coopera-tion which has so long been interrupted. The cause of it originated with the Trustees and it rests with them to remove it'. The Trustees, of course, hotly denied that any fault or blame lay with them, but all work at the Harbour was suspended, and steps taken for the complete close-down of operations. Among other things, one of the diving bells was sold to Portrush Harbour for £650, and John Fox was given notice of the termination of his contract, to expire on 25 December 1831.

Representatives of the ship owners and ships' masters sent a petition to the Trus-tees in September 1831 requesting that a lighthouse be built on the new west pier, and that work should commence on a new north wall. The petitioners agreed that, although the new pier had succeeded in improving conditions in the inner Harbour, it had also increased the difficulty in approaching the Harbour at times when the wind was between south-south-east and south-west. The Trustees provided two 120-fathom hawsers to be kept on the North Wall for the assistance of vessels entering the Harbour, and said that they would build a lighthouse 'as soon as the Consent of the Lord of the Manor can be obtained to its being done'. They also agreed that a new north wall was necessary, but pleaded lack of sufficient funds and 'difficulty in borrowing money in consequence of Lord Lonsdale and some of the Trustees having declined to join in executing the necessary securities'.

An order was eventually given on 16 February 1832 for the erection of a lighthouse 'with a small building 8' x 6' to be built 19 feet from the extremity of the West Pier'. Reluctant approval from Lonsdale had been obtained only after pointing out to him that he and the Trustees would be held responsible for any loss of life or property resulting from the lack of a lighthouse. When notifying his agreement, Lonsdale wrote on 22 November 1831, 'In ceasing to take any part in the deliberations of the Trustees, I was acutely under the impression that after the opinion they have been pleased to express of my individual conduct, my presence would no longer be useful'. The Trustees passed no comment, but ordered a lighthouse, an adjoining building and other work.

By the middle of 1832 the Trustees considered that Harbour developments were complete and began to repay their debts by redeeming some of the Harbour Bonds.

19   The Lighthouse, West Pier.

By 1830, Lonsdale had ceased to attend meetings of the Trustees, and merely responded to requests for approval of decisions as was required by the existing Acts. However, the Trustees were anxious not to alienate Lord Lonsdale completely, as he was still a very influential figure representing the interests of Whitehaven. He attended only one further meeting of the Board when, in 1836, he formally moved the adoption of the plans for the building of the ogee head to complete the West Pier. However, the link between the Board and members of the Lowther family was not completely severed: Lord Lowther, Lonsdale's heir, served as an elected Trustee during the 1820s and 1830s, although he did not attend many meetings.

The New North Pier

Sir John Rennie, in his annual report for 1830, noted that deposits of sand were forming near the baths and the New Quay, but made no specific recommendations. Instead he advised the Trustees to proceed with the building of a new North Pier— 'being in the shelter of the New West Pier it will be comparatively easy and cheap to build, and will give a stronger current into and out of the Harbour which will thus tend to increase the depth and carry away matter which might deposit itself into the Main or Offing Current and thus be carried out to sea'.

The Trustees approved plans to extend the North Wall at an estimated cost of £33,050, and Lord Lonsdale added his agreement on 3 April 1833. A resident engineer, David Logan, was appointed at a salary of £300 per annum. Logan had to employ and pay his own foreman, find his own house, and was not to be absent from the works except with the approval of the Trustees.

The new wall was to have two cants, the first in a straight line 1,120 feet in length from the end of the existing wall, and the second 125 feet in length at an angle of 142 degrees to the first. The pier was to terminate with a round head 60 feet in diameter. There were to be two flights of stairs to allow access to the pier from boats, two landing places, and the pier was to be completed with parapets eight feet high on the first cant, and 10 feet high on the second. The overall width of the New Pier was to be 40 feet.

Stone was obtained from the Bransty Quarries. The workmen there were paid 4d. to 9d. per cubic yard depending on the conditions, a rate which was calculated to enable a good workman to earn 2s. to 2s. 5d. per day. The stones were loaded by the same men onto waggons by crane at 4d. per waggon, which were then moved over the waggonway, again at 4d. per waggon, to the head of the North Wall.

The work proceeded at a rapid pace and, with the use of a diving bell to facilitate the laying of the foundations, some 140 yards were built to a height of 16 feet in the first season.

During construction, however, it became obvious that in normal bad weather conditions, the pier was not, after all, in the shelter of the New West Pier. Rennie commented that this was because the West Pier had not been completed as designed! An additional 32 yards were needed, finishing in a circular head. Rennie also recommended that the North Pier should incorporate a jetty built at right angles to the main structure, as in the design proposed in 1814.

All went well until 24 January 1836, when Whitehaven Harbour was subjected to the most severe storm ever recorded. Terrifying difficulties were encountered by several vessels attempting to enter the Harbour. Several ships were stranded near Redness Point while the brig *Musgrave* was totally destroyed, the smack *Belfast* was almost lost, and the smack *Hero* went aground, all three being driven by the storm on to the partially built head of the North Wall.

Public clamour demanded that the head and jetty be taken down immediately, as they were seen to be the cause of the destruction. However, calmer influences prevailed, John Peile suggesting that Sir John Rennie should be sent for and asked to comment on the situation. Lord Lonsdale and Lord Lowther were also invited to attend 'a meeting with Rennie and the Trustees on this momentous occasion'.

Rennie commented, somewhat bitterly, that the fault lay with the Trustees for not having completed the West Pier as envisaged in the plans of 1823. He pointed out that the head of the North Pier was intercepting the seas, which would have been deflected by the head of the West Pier if it had been built. He also pointed out that the *Musgrave* had been lost because her rigging had become entangled with a temporary crane on the jetty, and that, though with difficulty and some damage, all the other ships had eventually reached safety. Rennie also commented that he thought it most unfair that both piers were being condemned before either of them had been completed.

As a result, Logan produced plans for a massive circular head for the West Pier, which would deflect the running sea away from the Harbour entrance. Lord Lonsdale's feelings can be imagined when, on 30 August 1836, he formally moved the adoption of these plans.

The jetty and the head of the North Pier were first demolished, and work then began on the head of the West Pier. In March 1838, Logan wrote that work was almost completed, and he was about to commence on the northern side. Unfortunately, Logan died a few months afterwards, and the Trustees appointed Ebenezer Stiven as engineer.

It was next decided to demolish the North Pier back to the cant, and, using Logan's plans, to rebuild in a westerly direction in order that the head should be in the correct position relative to the head of the West Pier. Lord Lonsdale wrote on 31 December 1839: 'I have great satisfaction in concurring with the majority of the Trustees on this resolution, and if it is agreeable to usage, I should wish to have my approbation of it recorded'. Sir John Rennie was given notice that his services were no longer required, and the work was undertaken by Stiven. The pier, adorned with its crenellated lighthouse, was completed without further interruption in 1841.

Both piers, costing altogether some £150,000, were financed from annual income and by borrowings against Harbour Bonds. Throughout the period the bank accounts were never overdrawn. By 1841 the average annual income had risen to £8,000 per annum, a level which would have allowed the Trustees to repay the existing debts within 10 years or so.

The completed piers were found to be most successful in the purpose for which they were built. The ogee head of the West Pier prevented the sea from sweeping across the entrance to the Harbour, and it was found that ships could approach and enter the Harbour in all conditions of weather. In addition, the inner Harbour was now tranquil at all times.

The outer Harbour took 25 years to build but, after many trials along the way, it was finally complete. Gibson, of the

20   The Lighthouse, North Pier, *c.*1905.

21   Entrance and Pier. The pier on the right is the North Pier, the other is the West Pier.

Cumberland Pacquet, proudly announced that the new harbour was considered to be 'One of the most magnificent undertakings ever grappled with in this or perhaps any other part of the British Empire'.

Tragically, however, the new outer Harbour was not a commercial success, as the ships' masters were reluctant to use it. As early as March 1840, and before the completion of the North Pier, the Trustees formed a sub-committee to ascertain the legality or otherwise of charging reduced duties and commodity rates for vessels using the new piers, in order to encourage their use. Also, the Trustees would have preferred the new Steam Pacquet Company to use the New West Pier, but the steamer operators insisted on mooring at the Old Tongue. There were even discussions about shortening the New Tongue in order to facilitate access for the paddle steamers!

By mid-century, Whitehaven Harbour's income was growing only slowly, as the following figures for the year ended 25 March 1849 show:

INCOME				EXPENDITURE			
Tonnage Duties	3158	14	6	Harbour	3373	15	1
Merchandise Dues	1928	0	3	Costs of Steam Tug	588	14	1
Ballast	1195	11	6	Dredger & Hoppers	5924	8	6
Lamp Tonnage	322	16	6	Interest on Bonds	2359	10	6
	6605	2	9				
Steam Tug	684	5	4				
Other Incomes	193	13	8				
Bank Interest (Net)	7	9	10				
	7490	11	7				
Shortfall	4755	16	7				
£12246	8	2		£12246	8	2	

It will be seen that roughly one-third of total income was payable as interest to the bondholders.

However, a tidal harbour is always attended with serious inconveniences and, almost immediately, the Trustees began discussions with several eminent engineers for the provision of a wet dock. Many years were to elapse before their plans came to fruition.

The 1840s and 1850s were crucial years in the development of Whitehaven Harbour. The main problems were caused by the arrival of the railways, the demand for bigger ships, and the development of the iron ore trade. The railway from the north, the Whitehaven Junction Railway, opened in February 1847 and had its terminus at Bransty. That from the south, the Whitehaven and Furness Junction Railway, was opened throughout in November 1850, and its terminus, Newtown, was built in Preston Street. At first neither line was linked to the Harbour, nor was there a link between the termini.

22   The crest of the Whitehaven Junction Railway. Salvaged from the door of a first-class railway carriage, this panel is now in Whitehaven Museum.

The WJR built a Harbour branch, in 1848, to the North Wall, thus providing for the movement of goods both on and off vessels using North Harbour. The Trustees were required to deepen that part of the Harbour and also to strengthen the Wall.

It was recognised from the beginning that Whitehaven's two railway stations should be linked to each other, and in 1850, in order to do this, the W&FJR proposed to build a tramway through the streets of the town. The route chosen was to pass from Newtown, through the market place, along Strand Street and Tangier Street to Bransty. The scheme was strongly opposed by the owners and occupiers of properties along the route, and by the farmers using the market place. The Trustees voted overwhelmingly to reject the scheme. A second proposed route, this time via Newtown, Irish Street, Scotch Street, George Street, and Tangier Street was also rejected.

However, construction of a more satisfactory link between the two stations was already in hand. The W&FJR had decided that the best solution was to build a tunnel under the town. The tunnel was difficult to construct because of old coal workings, and also because Lord Lonsdale insisted that trains should not be visible from Whitehaven Castle, but it was eventually opened for traffic in September 1852. A new station was built by the W&FJR at Corkickle for passenger traffic, a development which reduced the use of the Preston Street station until the opening of the market place tramway.

Exploitation of the iron ore deposits in the Cleator area began in earnest during the 1840s. The very high quality of the ore soon created a large demand, and the building of the Whitehaven, Cleator and Egremont railway enabled huge quantities to be moved to Whitehaven to be shipped to iron-producing centres in Wales and Scotland.

Thomas Ainsworth of the Flosh, Cleator, one of the principal iron masters of the time, in 1852 placed a large screw-driven steamship on the Cardiff, Liverpool and Whitehaven route. His wish was to export iron ore and to import salt, and he asked permission to build sheds on the North Wall for the purpose. The Trustees refused his request, and Ainsworth was forced to use the Sugar Tongue, the ships being loaded from horse drawn carts. Later, Ainsworth introduced a bigger steamer of over 400 tons, and for this ship he demanded to be allocated a guaranteed berth, protection for the cargoes, and that the Harbour should be deepened. Again the Trustees refused on

23 Preston Street goodsyard in the 1970s. This was the Whitehaven Terminus of the Whitehaven and Furness Junction Railway, opened in 1850. These sheds give an indication of the size of operations in Victorian times.

the grounds that the Harbour had been deepened as far as was prudent. This incident illustrates that Whitehaven Harbour was already inadequate for the larger steam driven vessels then being built.

In 1855, the Whitehaven, Cleator and Egremont Railway was under construction for the specific purpose of transporting ore and pig iron to Whitehaven for onward shipment. The new line joined the W&FJR at Mirehouse, whence, over W&FJR metals, the trains were to travel through the tunnel and then over the WJR Harbour Branch to the shipping drops on North Wall. However, the W&FJR insisted on providing a special engine for travelling through the tunnel, for which they made a charge of 2s. for each train. In order to circumvent this irritation the WC&ER applied to the Trustees for access to the South Harbour.

After several false starts, permission was given to build a tramway through Newtown, the market place, Custom House Quay and so on to the Sugar (Old) Tongue. Because of the adjudged importance of this traffic, the Trustees even considered building two wooden jetties and moving the Lime (New) Tongue nearer to the Bulwark to make room for them. The new tramway was closed from 7 a.m. to 3 p.m. on market days, and the waggons were required to be horse drawn. The WC&ER brought many thousand tons of ore to Preston Street, whence, by the 1860s, over 400 waggons per day trundled their way to the Sugar Tongue.

The Search for a Wet Dock

Because of developments at Silloth, Workington and Barrow, all of which were vehemently opposed by the Trustees, it became apparent that, unless a wet dock was provided, Whitehaven would be superseded by the other ports.

In 1854, therefore, James Rendel was asked to design a comprehensive redevelopment of the Harbour which would include a wet dock and alterations to incorporate the railways. Rendel proposed to build a wall from Redness Point to the North Pier which would enclose almost 30 acres, of which about five would be devoted to a wet dock. Land access was to be provided from a new road to be built from Bransty Arch between the shipbuilding yards and the railway station. The Bulwark was also to be altered to improve railway access. The estimated cost of the scheme, £90,760, was considered too great an outlay. Rendel next proposed a plan for moving the Lime Tongue nearer to the Bulwark and building a wooden jetty in front of Custom House Quay. This also was thought to be too expensive.

The Trustees approved a plan to construct two wooden jetties in North Harbour. Each was to be 300 feet long, with one parallel to and 65 feet from the bulwark, and the other parallel to and 100 feet from the North Pier. Work was not started on this development however, and the Trustees eventually opted for the simplest and cheapest solution, the extension of the railway by the WJR along the bulwark. Within 12 months, allegedly because of financial constraints, plans for a comprehensive redevelopment of Whitehaven Harbour, which would have brought it up to date, were reduced to the laying of a railway track along one of the piers, with a viaduct to carry it over part of North Harbour. At first glance it would seem that the Trustees missed a great opportunity to reinstate Whitehaven as the leading port in the area, but it must be recognised that they had to work within strict financial limits.

In 1857, Alexander Meadows Rendel and George Rendel were appointed engineers to the Harbour with a brief to develop a wet dock. They produced several schemes—two in North Harbour, one between the Sugar Tongue and the Lime Tongue, and one between the Old and New Piers. The estimated cost of all these plans was in excess of the £70,000 which the Trustees were prepared to allocate. Indeed, the lowest of 10 tenders for one of the North Harbour schemes was for more that £113,000. Eventually, the Rendels were dismissed, and the search for a site for a wet dock was temporarily abandoned.

The Act of 1858

At the end of this period, the Trustees felt that their financial position was insufficiently secure, as bondholders could require repayment of their holding on demand.

A short Act of Parliament was obtained, therefore, to enable the Trustees to issue bonds for a fixed period of time.

However, for several years before 1858, pressure was being exerted by the rate-payers of Whitehaven for representation on the Board of the Trust. This resulted in a further Act of Parliament, that of 1859, which was to be a milestone in the history of the town.

Chapter 10

Town Administration and
Acts of Parliament 1859-1876

The continuing rivalries between the 'Town' and 'Castle' parties in Whitehaven is evidence of a significant element among the population opposed to control by the Lowther family. Of more importance at the time, however, was the national political situation, as the people began to find expression for their views and sympathies.

During the late 1820s, there was widespread national agitation for parliamentary reform, including an increase in suffrage. Whitehaven, seen by many as the most important town in the area, was not separately represented in the House of Commons. There were six seats in Cumberland, two for the county, two for Carlisle, and two for Cockermouth. Lonsdale nominated four of the six Members, and thus required them to vote in the Tory interest.

The Tories, of course, were strongly opposed to any reform of Parliament, their leader, the Duke of Wellington, considering the existing system to be as perfect as could be achieved. The people of Cumberland, however, voted for reform. At the 1831 general election, Lord Lowther, Lonsdale's heir, standing for one of the Cumberland seats, among the safest in the country, was heavily defeated, finishing a poor third. This result triggered the famous Whitehaven Riots of 1831.

Many of the prominent people of Whitehaven strongly supported the Whigs, and several of them were members of the Board of Trustees. Among them was William Miller (tanner), for many years chairman of the Board, Milham and Thomas Hartley (rope makers and bankers), William Randleson (druggist) and several others. These men saw themselves as disenfranchised as a result of Lord Lonsdale's activities, and consequently expressed their disapproval of the situation by consistently opposing every measure proposed by the ruling Tory group at meetings of the Trustees.

At the tri-annual election of Trustees held in 1832, the following were voted on to the board: Lord Lowther, Alexander Spitall, James Brockbank, Robert Jefferson, William Younghusband and John Harrison.

As a result of the Reform Act of 1832, Whitehaven became a separate constituency, and at the ensuing general election, as is shown in the Whitehaven Poll Book, all the members voted for Matthias Attwood, the Tory candidate. Indeed, Attwood was sponsored by Jefferson and Harrison.

The remaining eight elective Trustees, William Miller, Richard Barker, Milham Hartley, William Randleson, Thomas Hartley, Joseph Watson, George Harrison and Anthony Steel all voted for Isaac Littledale, the Whig candidate. Littledale was sponsored by Thomas Hartley and Richard Barker.

Thus exactly half of the elective Trustees were opposed to Lonsdale on political grounds.

Work on the West and North Piers continued throughout the 1830s but with great difficulty. New works required the approval of Lonsdale and 17 other Trustees, but the necessary majority could be found only very rarely. Indeed, the ruling group occasionally had difficulty in raising a simple majority. Whereas in 1802 the then Trustees expressed the wish to concur with Lord Lonsdale's wishes, the 1830s group felt strong enough to ignore his views, and to take decisions contrary to his wishes.

Lord Lonsdale appeared once more in Whitehaven when in 1836, aged 78 years, he formally proposed the building of the West Pier Head. That particular day must have given him a great deal of satisfaction! From this time, Lord Lonsdale and his son were only very rarely involved in the affairs of the town and Harbour. Communication between them and the Trustees was on a formal basis only. They were kept fully informed of the actions of the Trustees, but were only approached when approval was required by Acts of Parliament. Indeed, the evidence suggests that the Lonsdales, particularly the son, Lord Lowther, began to look to Workington for future developments. Jointly with Curwen of Workington Hall, an Act of Parliament was obtained in 1840 for the improvement of the town and harbour there, and a Board of Trustees was set up, of which Lord Lonsdale was a permanent member. As a result of the coming of the railways, and the development of the iron ore trade, the Lonsdales built an ironworks, and a wet dock at Oldside, Workington, both of which were in operation by 1865.

After Lord Lowther succeeded as 2nd Earl, following the death of his father in 1844, his brother Henry Cecil Lowther also served as an elected Trustee. He too attended very few meetings. Henry Cecil, however, was better known as the 'Silent Colonel'. He joined the army in 1807, and served under Wellington in the Peninsular War, eventually being promoted to the rank of Lieutenant-Colonel of the 12th Foot. He served as M.P. for Westmorland from 1812 until 1867, and during those years made only one speech in the House of Commons.

As the 2nd Earl had no legitimate offspring, on his death in 1872 the title passed to Henry, son of Henry Cecil. Before becoming 3rd Earl, Henry, like other members of his family, served for many years in the House of Commons. He was member for West Cumberland from 1847 until 1872. This Lord Lonsdale played no part at all in the affairs of the Board of Trustees.

His son, St George Henry, became 4th Earl at the age of 20, but died aged only 27 in 1882. However, he attended one meeting of the Trustees on 22 June 1881. After

24 The yacht *Northumbria*. This yacht was owned by Sir George Henry, 4th Earl of Lonsdale, and was in Whitehaven on 22 June 1882, when the Trustees of the Town and Harbour were entertained to dinner aboard.

the meeting, he entertained the Trustees to dinner aboard his yacht, *Northumbria*, which was anchored in Whitehaven Harbour. After his death, the Lonsdale Estates passed into the hands of Trustees and from 1882 the annual Nomination of Trustees was signed accordingly. The list for 1882 was signed by the Rt. Hon. James Lowther, M.P. for Redcar, and William Stuart Stirling Crawford of 45 Belgrave Square. This James Lowther, was a second cousin once removed of St George Henry and his brother and successor, Hugh Cecil, the legendary 5th Earl.

Hugh Cecil, the 5th Earl of Lonsdale was chosen as the first mayor of Whitehaven in 1894, and he presented the mace and mayoral chain to the Corporation.

Political matters again assumed great importance during the 1840s. When the Conservative government, led by Sir Robert Peel, repealed the Corn Laws in 1846, several of Whitehaven's leading figures immediately changed their political affiliations. Among these was Henry Jefferson, wine and spirits merchant. Formerly a Tory and supporter of the Lonsdale interest, Jefferson assumed the role of leader of the Whig group and led them to victory in the election of 1850. Jefferson easily topped the poll, and for the first time the Whigs formed a majority of the elected Trustees.

The victors were accused of unscrupulous behaviour at the election. The only polling station in the town was at the public office in Lowther Street (the site of the present post office) and, allegedly, the Whig supporters blocked Lowther Street at its

Olden Whitehaven — Old Public Offices, Lowther Street

25   The old Public Offices. The town's main post office now stands on this site.

junctions with Queen Street and Scotch Street, thus ensuring that many Tory supporters, especially the females, were unable to cast their votes. Regardless of the validity of
these allegations, separate polling places were provided for the ladies at following
elections, in order 'to avoid the disgraceful scenes' of 1850!

Although the Whigs held the balance of power, the Rev. Henry Lowther, an elected
Tory, became chairman of the Trustees, and under his guidance, there began the
committee system of running Whitehaven's affairs. The first committees were Water,
Harbour, Police and Street, Audit and Finance, and Cupola.

The purpose of the Cupola committee was to acquire the building in Duke Street
(known as the Cupola), for the use of the Trustees. It was to provide living accommodation for the police inspector and unmarried constables, magistrates offices and session
house, a house of correction and a board room for the Trustees. After purchase, the
building continued to be known as the Cupola, and it was not until February 1853, that
it was formally resolved to call it the 'Town Hall'.

Before the Reform Act of 1832, the national government did not become involved
in matters of a local nature in the country but, in the following years, a large number
of measures were introduced affecting the organisation of local government, especially
in the area of public health.

The Board of Trustees had operated within the terms of the many Acts of Parliament specific to Whitehaven, but the passing of measures such as the Removal of

Nuisances Act 1846, and particularly of the Public Health Act 1848, brought new responsibilities, among them the provision of a water supply. As the local authority for the area, the Trustees obtained the Whitehaven Waterworks Act 1849, and at last an adequate supply of high quality, potable water was brought from Ennerdale Lake to the town and Harbour. The work was carried out under the supervision of Thomas Hawksley, an eminent civil engineer, and was completed in 1852, at a cost in excess of £21,000.

Immediately before the passing of the Waterworks Act, the rates in the town were levied at 2s. in the pound in order to pay for the improvements carried out under the Act of 1816. Largely as a result of the further rate of 1s. in the pound required for the water supply, the ratepayers of Whitehaven demanded representation in the government of the town.

The year 1859 was one of particular importance in the history of Whitehaven Harbour. The Trustees by this time were under severe pressure to improve and to increase the facilities required by the users of the Harbour. The tonnage of iron ore had increased rapidly, as had that of coal. The shippers demanded deep water berths, which were not available and, in addition, the access to the Harbour for the railways was totally inadequate. Developments had taken place at Silloth, Maryport, and Barrow which were endangering the importance of Whitehaven as a port. Also, there was the problem of the long lasting dispute with Lord Lonsdale, and the rights of the Trustees over the land adjacent to North Harbour.

In order, therefore, to tackle these problems, it was decided to instruct the solicitor to the Board, William Lumb, to prepare a Bill for a new Act of Parliament. A committee of seven members of the Board was formed to confer with the Lord of the Manor 'as to the best mode of preparing the Bill'.

The Act of 1859

The result, after many meetings and debates, was the Act of 1859 (22 Vict Cap 17): 'An Act for transferring the Government of the new Limits of the Harbour of Whitehaven to the Harbour Trustees, for making better Provision for the Election of Trustees, and for the Alteration of Rates and Duties ...'. It contained the following provisions:

The disputed land, described in the Act of 1792, was transferred to the Trustees, and they were given full rights and powers equal to those held over other parts of the Harbour.

Those provisions of the preceding Acts which required the approval or consent of the Lord of the Manor were repealed, thus enabling the Trustees to act on their own, without consulting Lord Lonsdale.

While it was recognised that, as Lord of the Manor, Lonsdale held certain rights over the Harbour, and consequently had a material interest in its management, it was nevertheless decided that his potential influence on the Board should be reduced. Lonsdale (or his deputy) continued as a permanent Trustee, but the number of his nominees was reduced from six to five, and the elective Trustees increased from fourteen to fifteen. For the first time, also, ratepayers were eligible to vote at elections.

The town was divided into five wards, with three elected Trustees for each: St James, St Nicholas, Trinity, Newtown and Harbour. The boundaries of the wards were described in detail. As an example, that of St Nicholas reads:

> St Nicholas Ward comprises those Parts of the Town which are bounded by a Line commencing at the South East Corner of Roper Street; thence proceeding along the Centre of Scotch Street to the Centre of Duke Street; thence along the centre of Duke Street in a Northerly Direction to the South West End of Duke Street near the Bulwark; thence in a Westerly Direction between the Town and Harbour as far as the East Strand; thence along East Strand, across the Market Place, and along the Centre of Roper Street to the Point first named.

Those persons entitled to vote in an election of Trustees were:

(1)   The Master of any Vessel registered at Whitehaven, who had resided within the limits of the Parliamentary Borough for Six Months preceding 1 September 1859.

(2)   Every Person owning not less than Four Sixtyfourth Shares of any such Vessel, who had owned the Shares for at least sixth months prior to 1 September 1859, and who also fulfilled the residential qualification.

(3)   Every Person residing within the Limits of the Wards, occupying any House, Shop, Office, Counting House, Warehouse or other Building situated within any of the Wards. Provided that any such Person was, in respect of such occupation rated at a net annual rateable Value of not less than Six Pounds per Annum, in the Rate in force for the Relief of the Poor, and was so rated for Six Months prior to 1 September 1859.

Any person could stand for election as a Trustee, provided he resided within seven miles from the Parliamentary Boundary of the borough. He could stand for any of the wards, whether he lived within its limits or not.

The new Act required that, at the time of elections, polling stations were to be provided in each of the wards. They were situated in the following locations in 1859:

(1)   St James Ward - At a Booth to be erected in Duke Street at the Corner of High Church Street.

(2) St Nicholas - At the Public Office, Lowther Street.

(3) Trinity - At the Town Hall, Duke Street.

(4) Newtown - At a Booth to be erected adjoining Mr Trohear's Shop in the Newtown.

(5) Harbour - At the Refuge School in the Market Place.

Each ward had a presiding officer (one of the Trustees) and two inspectors of votes. Elections were to be held annually, and the date was moved from August to November.

Fifteen Trustees were elected in November 1859. The Trustee in each ward who received the least number of votes was to retire at the end of the first year, and the next lowest at the end of two years. Thereafter annual elections were held, with each Trustee being elected for a three-year term. Henry Jefferson, who had led the Whigs in 1850, and had failed in the elections of 1853 and 1856, scraped in as one of the Trustees for St Nicholas ward! In fact virtually all the Trustees from the old Board were re-elected.

The Trustees were required to maintain those facilities used in the interests of Lord Lonsdale for the export of coals, and also to provide similar facilities, in the shape of hurries, chutes, etc., on any new docks to be built. A revised list of duties and charges came into force on 1 August 1859, and the Trustees had powers to change them as they found necessary.

The first revised election of Trustees took place in November 1859, and the new Board immediately created a number of committees, each of which was made responsible for a specific aspect of the various affairs of the town and Harbour. These were the 'Harbour, Wet Dock, Water and Street and Sanatory [sic]' committees. They also agreed that the provisions of the Local Government Acts of 1858 and 1861 should be applied to Whitehaven and, as a first move, they appointed Robert Lumb as the Medical Officer of Health at a salary of £50 per annum.

They also invited Thomas Hawksley to design a sewage scheme for the town. The new sewers were to extend:

(1) To the Cemetery on the Low Road to St Bees.

(2) To the Hensingham Toll Bar.

(3) To the Arch under Lord Lonsdale's private Carriage Road above Hilton Terrace.

(4) To the Bransty Railway Station.

(5) To Duke Pit Gate at the Top of Mount Pleasant.

(6) To the Coach Road leading from Corkickle to the Ginns.

The work was carried out by Messrs Newell and Ducross, at a cost of £21,741.

It was recognised that the most urgent requirement for the Harbour was a wet dock, and Rendel was again approached for plans for a five-acre scheme between the

Old and New Quays. The plans, when produced, were rejected, again because of the cost. The Trustees were determined that Whitehaven should have a wet dock, but a further scheme by Rendel, sited near William Pit, and one by Sir John Coode on Wellington Beach were also rejected. It seemed that it was not possible to produce a suitable scheme within the means of the Trustees, and in mid-1866 the search for a wet dock was again abandoned.

However, in the interim, and in order to ease the situation for iron ore shipments, George Burrell, the harbour engineer, proposed to build a wooden jetty in North Harbour. The jetty was to be 300 feet in length, 31 feet wide, and 15 feet above high water at spring tides. Its position was to be parallel to and 100 feet from the North Wall. The jetty, provided with three lines of rails, was to be connected to the existing railway serving the Bulwark, and would provide five additional berths for ore vessels. Work began on the jetty in March 1860, and it was completed in June 1862 at a cost of a little over £3,100. The Trustees insisted that the WJR supplied the pointwork for the railway connection, and that the WC&ER paid for the iron spouts used in the discharge of the ore in to the ships.

There was a great deal of concern, in 1868, about the financial status of the Board of Trustees, and an investigation into expenditure was carried out. In the first place, the investigators had the greatest difficulty in obtaining the relevant information, as some of the accounts were four years in arrears! Accounting practices were, to say the least, imaginative. Interest payments were charged to capital (a common practice at the time), and it was found that estimates of income had been made on the most optimistic bases; for example, town rate income was calculated without allowing for non-payments and for property standing empty. Allowance was made for rate income in respect of the Harbour, although it had never been assessed to rates, nor had any ever been paid.

At the time the Board had a total bonded debt of £120,678. Of this £44,052 was in respect of the Harbour (some of which dated back to 1829), £46,170 in respect of the waterworks, and £30,456 in respect of the sewerage system. Great alarm was expressed at the amount of interest payable (for the Harbour this amounted to some £2,009 annually), and also at the way in which operating costs of all the services were increasing.

It was found, for instance, that the wage rates paid to Trust employees were higher than those available elsewhere in Whitehaven, and also that bought materials were more expensive than was necessary. It was decided to close down the Harbour workshops and to purchase all future work and materials by tender.

It was also found to be extremely difficult to enforce the scale of duties on commodities moved through the Harbour, as no duties were charged at the neighbouring ports of Harrington, Workington and Maryport. In fact, several of the Whitehaven traders imported goods through Workington as, even after adding the cost of rail transport, goods still arrived cheaper at Whitehaven. Because of this, the Trustees felt obliged to reduce the duties to 25 per cent of the rates imposed by the Act of 1859. Many other remedial actions were taken, including the proper charging for services such as the supply of water to shipping, and the letting of the Market Hall and Town Hall. Another drive for the collection of unpaid rates was also undertaken. Much disapproval was also expressed at the very low level of attendance of Trustees at meetings of the Board. A register of attendance was introduced to monitor that each member fulfilled his obligations.

A great deal of money had been spent on the Harbour during this period, particularly on dredging, in order to keep it functioning adequately; after taking running expenses into account, the annual income was found to be insufficient to make a significant reduction of the debt, let alone to take on additional commitments. Nevertheless, because of the volume of minerals passing through the port, pressure for a wet dock continued, and the Trustees felt justified in instructing their harbour engineer, David Stiven, to draw up plans for a dock in North Harbour, to be sited in front of the shipbuilding yards. Stiven's plans were sent to Mr. Brunlees, a consultant, for approval. After some amendment, they were approved by the Board on 24 January 1870, with work to commence as soon as possible.

The Act of 1871

The Whitehaven Dock and Railways Act 1871 (34 & 35 Vict Cap 91) empowered the Trustees to build a wet dock 'partly in the present North Harbour, partly in the shipbuilding yard in the occupation of the Whitehaven Shipbuilding Co Ltd, and partly in lands situated between the present North Harbour and Tangier Street'. This plan required the removal of the existing old North Wall and the building of a new one, and also the removal of the wooden jetty.

In order to provide proper railway access to the new dock, two railways were included in the scheme. The first ran from the first coal hurry on West Strand to the Bulwark, where it connected with the existing WJR (by now L&NWR) branch. The second was a short link from the Old (Sugar) Tongue to the existing W&FJR (by now Furness) in front of the Custom House. The first railway crossed the patent slip, and a swing bridge was required in order that the slip could continue in operation.

The substantial parcel of land required for the overall scheme was owned by Lord Lonsdale. Following the death of William, the second Earl, in 1872, negotiations were concluded with his agents, and the land was eventually acquired for £10,516.

The Act of 1816 had given borrowing powers totalling £180,000, and this was confirmed in the 1871 Act. However, of the monies borrowed, only £75,000 was to be spent on the new dock and railways. Ten tenders were received from various firms

26   A view across the Harbour from the *Grand Hotel.*

27   Haig Pit.

28   Old harbour offices before the building of extensions, *c.*1890.

interested in the work, the lowest being for £65,232, and the highest £138,500! Brunlees recommended the acceptance of the tender from Walter Scott of Newcastle at £69,743, but the Trustees chose instead that from Joseph Phillips at £75,869. Three years into the work, Phillips retired and assigned the contract to Parry, Kirk and Knight. Work on the new dock began in early 1872 and, although always behind schedule, continued without serious interruption until its completion. The dock, named the Queen's Dock in honour of Queen Victoria, was opened with great éclat on 22 November 1876.

An important part of the new works was the construction of a sea wall between the Lime Tongue and the Bulwark. The railway from the Bulwark to the hurries was built on the strip of land resulting from the infilling behind it. In addition, new dock offices complete with 'sanatory conveniences' were built near the inward end of the Bulwark. These works, together with the swing bridge, were completed during 1877. By this time, however, the huge volumes of iron ore exports had begun to decline, and the short railway in front of the Customs House connecting with the market place tramway, together with the requisite widening of Custom House Quay, were still under consideration in 1888.

29   The swing bridge in 1913.

30   Whitehaven Customs House, erected in 1811, photographed *c*.1900. Prior to 1811 the customs officers were housed in other premises in the town. This building overlooking Custom House Dock was much more convenient.

Unfortunately, during the building period, the Trustees had been unable to borrow the necessary amount of money to pay for the new development. Investment in the Harbour Bonds had been slower than expected, and eventually the Bank of Whitehaven refused to meet their cheques. Attempts were made to borrow from other banks, and a deputation even went to London seeking suitable facilities.

The Act of 1876

The major object of this Act was to rationalise the financial position of the Board, and it embodied powers to borrow further amounts of money and to delay repayment of existing debts. By the time of the passing of the Act, the bonded debt in respect of the Harbour had risen to £85,531.

The Trustees were enabled to borrow £36,000 for the wet dock in addition to the £75,000 authorised by the Act of 1871, and also to borrow £10,500, to pay for a steam tug, *Whitehaven*, which they had had in operation for some time! Also they were allowed to extend the period of repayment of borrowed monies from 50 to 70 years. There were also clauses allowing the Trustees to levy tolls on the new railways, and also to increase most of the duties and charges then payable.

During the late 1870s, the dock railway (connected to Bransty) was extended underneath the hurries and along the West Pier, to which a branch was provided from Wellington Pit. A 'Grand Opening' of the new facilities was arranged in June 1880.

The year 1879 was a black one in the history of Whitehaven Harbour. First, the steam tug, *Whitehaven*, was sunk off the Isle of Man. Unfortunately, she was not insured, and the Trustees suffered a loss of £10,000. A few months later, the gates of the Queen's Dock ceased to function. This led to a dispute between the Trustees and the contractors over the final payments of the accounts, a claim for £12,810 being made. The case, which went to arbitration, resulted in an award being made against the Trustees. The problem of the dock gates was due probably to movement of the foundations, and extensive repairs at enormous cost were necessary before the dock could be reopened in 1882. During the intervening period Queen's Dock was operated as a tidal harbour.

The cost of the dock including the repairs was some £162,000. Already in straitened circumstances, the financial status of the Board of Trustees was now very serious. The bonded debt had risen to £177,446, the banks would not grant further credit, and indeed the position was reached when each Trustee was required to sign an individual guarantee in order that a cheque for £16,169, owing to Parry, Kirk and Knight in respect of the wet dock, could be issued.

It is most unfortunate that, during the last 25 years or so of the existence of the old Board, the Trustees were constantly beset by financial difficulties. From 1868, the position gradually deteriorated despite all their efforts to remedy the situation. There were frequent discussions with the various banks in the area over the amounts owing, during which various accounts were often switched between the Bank of Whitehaven, the Whitehaven Joint Stock Bank, and the Cumberland Union Banking Company. In 1875, the Trustees even resorted to advertising for money in the newspapers. In addition to those published in Whitehaven, advertisements were placed in the *Newcastle Journal*, the *Penrith Advertiser*, the *Kendal Mercury*, the *Lancaster Guardian* and the *Ulverston Advertiser*.

There was a great deal of dissension among the Trustees themselves over the handling of financial affairs, and in 1880 legal advice was taken 'on the advisability of applying for a writ of mandamus to compel Members of the Board to sign cheques and bonds and perform other administrative duties to carry out resolutions legally agreed upon by a Majority of Trustees'.

As can well be imagined, the state of affairs was a matter of public discussion, and most of it was critical of the Trustees. Consideration was given to suing the Whitehaven newspapers because of adverse comments made about the financial status and credit worthiness of the Board.

However, other matters were also pressing. As a result of the Public Health Act 1875, the Board of Trustees had become an Urban Sanitary Authority, and in order to obtain the extra powers required it was decided to seek incorporation.

Chapter 11

Incorporation 1885-94

The Act of 1885

As a result of the Whitehaven Town and Harbour (Incorporation) Act 1885 (48 & 49 Vict), the Board of Trustees became a body corporate with perpetual succession and a common seal.

The Harbour property was transferred to the name of the Board, and the Trustees were then able to mortgage the property and also to sell any they thought surplus to requirements. In lieu of borrowing money against bonds, the Trustees were empowered to issue debentures, the Whitehaven Harbour Debenture Stock, secured on the Harbour rates and duties.

Under this Act, the Trustees also took powers:
(1)   to build a graving dock between the swing bridge and the Bulwark.
(2)   to widen the Custom House Quay.
(3)   to widen the New Tongue.
(4)   to build a new sea wall between the New Quay and the West Pier.
(5)   to demolish the Fort and adjacent limekiln.

In order to carry out these works, additional borrowing powers for £80,000 were granted.

It seems almost incredible that, in view of their financial position, the Trustees should indulge in further expensive schemes. However, during the mid-1880s, the economy was again in severe recession, and although the graving dock and New (Lime) Tongue plans were shelved, all the other schemes were undertaken. The contemporary minutes of the Board make it clear that this was done largely to provide work for unemployed men, of whom there were large numbers in Whitehaven at the time. All the works were completed in the next five or six years. In addition, many hundreds of tons of sand and mud were dug by hand from the bed of the Harbour, as part of the ongoing work of maintaining its depth. Money to help to pay for this latter work was raised by public subscription. In July 1885, the Trustees were unable to pay the amount of the interest due on the Harbour Bonds. An arrangement was made with the Cumberland Union Banking Co. for a loan of £5,155, in return for a mortgage on the Town Hall and Duke Street properties.

The Common Seal of the Board arrived in August 1885, and its first use was on this mortgage deed. The inscription on the seal read: 'Seal of the Trustees of the Town and Harbour of Whitehaven. Established 1708 7 Queen Anne, Incorporated 1885, 49 Queen Victoria—"Persevere"'.

In September 1885, a receiver was appointed to look after the affairs of the Harbour 'in the interests of the Bondholders and of the Trustees', and two years later yet another Act of Parliament was required to 'regulate the rights of the Bondholders and other Creditors'. In 1887, the bonded debt in respect of the Harbour had reached the figure of £244,685. There was also a judgement debt due to the Cumberland Banking Co. Ltd. of £18,492, and other creditors of £1,508. The annual income at this time averaged £13,500 but, as the interest on the bonds was £10,500, and the annual yearly working expenses cost £5,000, there was a deficit increasing at the rate of £2,000 a year.

During this difficult period, the Trustees were drawn into many matters resulting from national legislation. Most were in the areas of public health and town planning. In 1879, for instance, they approved the plans for the Union Hall in Scotch Street, but in 1890 they turned down a scheme to convert an old sail cloth mill at Hensingham into '6 Dwelling Houses'.

As early as 1876, the Trustees were involved with smoke abatement, as in that year proceedings were threatened against Jackson's Timber Yard, Irish Street, for 'Smoke Nuisance'. They also went to great lengths to try to ensure that the Harbour steam tugs kept their smoke emissions to a minimum. The first use of a compulsory purchase order appears to have been in 1884, when certain property on Mount Pleasant, condemned by the medical officer of health as 'being unfit for Human Habitation', was bought for demolition. Also, a triangular piece of land 'opposite the Castle Hotel in Low Corkickle' was bought and the buildings cleared.

The Trustees had a more pleasant duty to perform on 15 May 1888, when they opened the Whitehaven Free Public Library in premises at 137 Queen Street. This followed from the passing of the Free Public Libraries Act 1880, and the new library was controlled by a committee of eight Trustees and seven ratepayers.

Among many other things, the Trustees were also responsible for issuing Petroleum Storage Licences (1869), the Inspection of Common Lodging Houses, the implementation of the Public House Closing Act (1869), the Dairies and Cowsheds Regulations, and the regulations regarding bad meat exposed for sale. They also had nominees on the School Attendance Committee, created under the Education Acts of the 1870s, and were involved with the rebuilding of the Infectious Diseases Hospital at Bransty, which resulted from the Infectious Diseases (Prevention) Act 1890.

By the 1890s, the Trustees were drawn from a variety of trades and professions, although it is noticeable that there were no clergymen among them. The full list of members of the Board of Trustees of the Town and Harbour before incorporation in 1894 was:

LONSDALE'S DEPUTY
William Little*   Hutton Hall, Penrith   Gentleman

LONSDALE'S NOMINEES
William Houlgate   67 Lowther Street   Bank Manager
Thomas Howson*   143 Queen Street   Solicitor
William McCowan   Roseneath, Moresby   Gentleman
Richard W Moore   4 Cross Street   Mining Engineer
Peter Shepherd   62 George Street   Gentleman

ELECTIVE TRUSTEES
John Atkinson JP   81 Lowther Street   Gentleman
James Baird *   10 Corkickle   Ironmaster
Thomas Bowman   5 Corkickle   Grocer
John Bragg   Cross Street   Ship Owner

31   This composite photograph is of the very last Board of Trustees of the Town and Harbour of Whitehaven, and it appeared in the *Whitehaven News* on 18 October 1894.

Jonathan Cant *	160 Queen Street	Gentleman
Richard Cousins	Coach Road	Brick and Tile Manufacturer
James G Dees CE JP	Floraville	Parkside Mining Co
Hamilton Dixon *	Royal Standard PH	Wines/Spirits Merchant
Wilson Hastwell	Bransty Villa	Pork Butcher etc
James Jacques	12 Inkerman	Gentleman
Thomas K Metcalfe *	9 Oakbank	Grocer
John Musgrave JP	2 Lowther Street	Retired Solicitor
John L Paitson	2 Foxhouses Road	Solicitor 2 Irish St
John Pattinson	Greenbank	Corn Merchant
Alexander Wilson	21 Corkickle	Photographer etc

* These six men also became members of the first Board of Harbour Commissioners: Little as Lonsdale's Deputy; Cant, Dixon and Metcalfe as nominees of the Town Council; Baird, elected to represent the traders and shipowners; Howson elected to represent the bondholders.

AY. OCTOBER 18, 1894.   5.

J. CANT. MR. J. L. PAITSON.   MR. A. WILSON.   MR. R. W. MOORE.   MR. T. K. METCALFE.
...SON.   LORD LONSDALE.   MR. J. ATKINSON. MR. R. COUSINS.   MR. J. BRAGG.   MR. W. HOLLGATE.

The Borough of Whitehaven

Throughout the 1880s, there had been increasing agitation in Whitehaven for the incorporation of the town as a borough. In 1888, the Trustees formed the Incorporation and Extension Committee, to examine the problems involved and ultimately to apply to the Privy Council for a charter of incorporation.

It was envisaged that the existing Board of Trustees would be divided into two bodies. One was to be the Borough of Whitehaven, with a corporation of aldermen and councillors, while the other, originally thought of as the 'Whitehaven Harbour and Dock Board' was to be created with its own board of commissioners.

The Trustees also took the opportunity to examine how best to extend the boundaries of Whitehaven, with a view to increasing substantially the rateable value of the new borough. Eventually, and after much discussion between Cumberland County Council, the Local Government Board, and the Trustees, new boundaries were agreed, and a large part of Preston Quarter was added to the town. The greater area of the new borough resulted in a sixth ward, Bransty, being created. The extension of the boundaries added only 845 to the population of 19,295, but the rateable value increased from £58,269 to £70,189.

The Borough of Whitehaven received its Charter of Incorporation on 20 July 1894 and, after the elections held in the following November, Hugh Cecil, 5th Earl of Lonsdale was elected as the first mayor.

There was a great deal of controversy, however, before the composition of the new Board of Harbour Commissioners was decided upon. The Trustees assumed that representatives of the new town council, with nominees appointed by Lord Lonsdale, would form the management of the new board. The bondholders, who by now had formed an association, thought differently, however. They claimed that, as they had supplied some £245,000 in order to complete the wet dock and other works, they were, therefore, the actual owners of the Harbour. Consequently they demanded at least one-third of the 15 seats on the new board. The Trustees, on the other hand, insisted that the bondholders were merely mortgagees of future Harbour dues and revenues and, as they already had legal remedy by foreclosing their mortgages, they were, therefore not entitled to any representation at all. After many meetings and consequent delay, it was eventually agreed that the Board of Harbour Commissioners would consist of four members nominated by Lord Lonsdale, four members nominated by Whitehaven Town Council, three members elected by the traders and ship owners, and four members elected by the bondholders a total of fifteen.

The Trustees and Innovation

The 19th century saw the development of many technological changes and innovations, including the introduction of the steam engine, railways, gas lighting, and later the telephone and electricity. The attitude of the Trustees to these changes is interesting, to say the least.

Throughout most of the century, the Trustees were involved in heavy expenditure on the Harbour, and after 1816 on town improvement. Particularly in the latter case, finance, although difficult, was never a severe problem, bearing in mind the low population of potential ratepayers, and the threat that the most affluent citizens would leave the town of Whitehaven for the surrounding area including Moresby, Hensingham and Egremont where rates were not payable. Throughout the period therefore, the Trustees pursued a policy of subletting work by contract, instead of undertaking the work 'in house'. In addition, this approach provided directorships for some of the Trustees in companies formed to carry out new ventures.

The supply of gas is a case in point. In early 1821, an enterprising individual suggested to the Trustees that, if they would build a gas works, he would manage it for them. The Trustees turned down this proposition, commenting that they would wait until a company was formed for the purpose. In fact it was not until 1830 that the Whitehaven Gas Light Company was created, and a gas works built on land owned by Lord Lonsdale adjoining William Pit. The oil lamps then used to light the streets were replaced by gas lights, and the Trustees accepted the gas company's offer to illuminate the town for one year for £367 4s. 7d. Some of the oil lamps were sold to Egremont, where at the time there was no street lighting. During the installation period, much fuss was made by the Board of Trustees over their inability to grant permission for the gas company to dig trenches in the streets as, although they owned the surface, the land underneath was owned by Lord Lonsdale. Lonsdale published a letter, heavy with sarcasm, in the *Cumberland Pacquet*. Was it likely, he asked, that having granted a lease for the ground on which to build the gasworks, he would then forbid the laying of the necessary pipework through the streets?

Late in 1839, by which time construction of the Maryport and Carlisle Railway had begun, the Trustees were asked to give their reaction to the extension of that railway to Whitehaven. The Trustees, on 3 December 1839, voted 'not to give an Answer'. The subsequent development of the railways in west Cumberland undoubtedly brought greater benefits to adjacent ports than to Whitehaven, but it is interesting to note that many of the Trustees became directors of the Whitehaven Junction, the Whitehaven and Furness Junction and later, the Whitehaven Cleator and Egremont Railways.

By 1864, a submarine telegraph line had been laid between Whitehaven and the Isle of Man. Because of the allegedly high cost, the Trustees declined to pay for weather forecasts to be transmitted along it. However, much more interest was shown in the telephone. In July 1881, a Mr. Butler proposed to install a telephone in the Harbour office and, a month later, an agreement was signed with Butler regarding 'a Telephonic Wire erected on the Sugar Tongue'. Later, in 1885, a further agreement with the

National Telephone Company was entered into regarding the erection of poles and wires.

In 1883, a firm named Hammond and Co. asked permission of the Trustees 'to light the Town using the Brush Electric Light'. The Trustees wrote to several towns, including Cockermouth, where electricity already had been installed, asking their experiences. Eventually, on 2 October 1883, the Board voted eight to six against the introduction of electricity to Whitehaven. Later, however, it was decided that the supply of electricity was one activity which could be operated to advantage by the Board of Trustees and, in 1890, an Electric Lighting Order was obtained. Plant generating electricity at 110 volts DC was installed in the sewerage pumping engine house on West Strand, and 450 electric street lamps were switched on for the first time on 1 September 1893. By the end of 1894, there were also 81 private consumers.

Although the steam engine was available for use throughout the 19th century, it was not until after the completion of Queen's Dock in 1876 that travelling steam cranes were first introduced to Whitehaven Harbour. In 1880, an attempt was made to extend the Harbour railway on to the Old Pier, and locomotives with vertical boilers and a short wheelbase were sought in order to negotiate the very sharp curve from West Strand. This project was eventually abandoned.

Conclusion

The fortunes of Whitehaven Harbour during the last 25 years or so of the 19th century declined quite dramatically. The Trustees were severely criticised for their

32   View of West Strand, Whitehaven Harbour.

33   The bucket dredger *Fleetwood* working in the Harbour in 1904.

mishandling of affairs and, although they cannot be held blameless, they were also caught up in a series of events over which they had little control.

The decline began with the introduction of the railways and the lack of access for them to the Harbour. The single track tunnel, built to link two railway systems, proved to be a serious bottleneck in the movement of minerals to the North Harbour, the only point of railway access. The delays involved encouraged the construction of other railways to Workington and places further north, thus depriving Whitehaven of much needed trade.

During the many years that the Trustees had spent trying to find a site for their wet dock, Barrow, Workington, Maryport and Silloth had completed facilities of their own. By the time Queen's Dock was operational, it became obvious that it was too small, that the entrance was too narrow to accommodate the larger vessels then being built and, most important of all, it came into use too late. By 1900, the Harbour was almost solely dependent on coal exports. The large quantities of iron ore previously shipped had ceased and, as no large scale industries had been founded in the area, little other trade was available.

Apparently, the Harbour at this time had a sad and neglected appearance. There was no water between the West and North Pier Heads at low tide, whereas in 1840, at the time of their completion, there had been a minimum of nine feet. Both the Outer and Inner Harbours required extensive dredging operations, having become

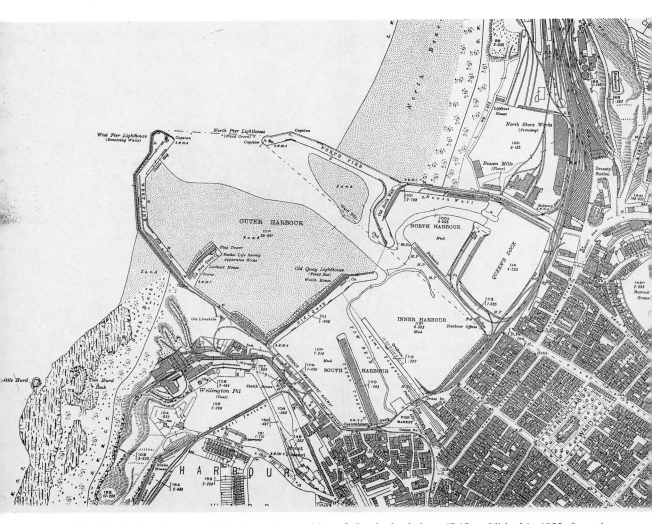

34   This is taken from an old Ordnance Survey Map of Cumberland sheet 67.02, published in 1925, from the survey of 1923.

severely silted up over the years. Some dredging was done in 1900, when some 72,000 tons of material were removed from the Outer Harbour alone. Only the Sugar Tongue and the coal hurries were in constant use; the Queen's Dock and Outer Harbour were used only occasionally by certain shippers. In addition, the Harbour was seriously in debt.

Chapter 12

Day by Day Operations—19th Century

Repairs and Maintenance

There can be little doubt that the Harbour was in a somewhat run down condition at the end of the 18th century. However, the dilapidations were remedied during the major rebuilding of the Harbour undertaken between 1804 and 1809.

By 1812, it was considered 'that the Repairs of the Piers being completed and the whole Harbour in good order, a considerable reduction in the present Establishment of Masons and Labourers may take place without Inconvenience to the Port'. The staff at that time consisted of seven masons, one smith, six labourers and one pick boy employed on the Harbour works, as well as one mason, two carpenters and one labourer under the direction of the pier master. The pier master was allowed to add two masons and one smith to his staff, but all the rest of the workmen were dismissed.

Every few years a report was made to the Trustees on the state of the Harbour and equipment. In 1821:

(1) New Quay—'In a perfect state or nearly so'. However a lighthouse was badly needed. The ships' masters complained that the lighthouse on the Old Quay was not visible from St Bees Head: a situation they had endured for over 75 years!

(2) Old Quay—the upright fenders and framing were reported to be in very bad state, 'affecting the security of the Pier'. The paving needed to be completed with square stone.

(3) Lime (New) Tongue—the framing and fenders needed a lot of attention. Projecting ironwork was dangerous to shipping.

(4) Old Tongue—the foundations were very unsafe, as the harbour bottom was found to be several feet below them.

(5) The Bulwark—there was a splay in the Bulwark which needed to be altered and the inner angle at the end of the North Wall needed to be made square.

(6) There was a vast accumulation of mud between the Old and New Tongues which should have been cleared by the hoppers.

(7) It was recommended that an office be built at the head of Old Quay 'for the Harbour Master on that Side'.

131

(8) It was desirable that the arches in Old Tongue, New Tongue and the Bulwark be built up.

Most of this work was done, as the report of 1833 shows. At that date, the Harbour Master reported that some of the framing and fenders needed replacing, but that no timber was available. No other structural repairs were required, but apparently there were large deposits of sand and mud to be cleared urgently. The Harbour Master also commented that, in his opinion, the Lime Tongue needed to be shortened by 10 yards, 'the better to accommodate the Steam Pacquets'. The state of other equipment was also reported on. The hoppers all required a great deal of work, while the Harbour boat was beyond repair; a new one being necessary. The fire engines 'have not been cleaned for a considerable time', and all the hoses and leather buckets were unserviceable. It is clear that these reports showed little more than fair wear and tear, and they were quickly acted on by the Trustees to maintain the Harbour and its equipment in good order.

By the 1830s, the Old (Sugar) Tongue had become the centre of activity at the Harbour. A great deal of goods and merchandise passed over it, and in order that cargoes would obtain some protection from the weather, a shed was built on the Quay 'for the general Accommodation of the Trade of the Port' in 1838. The shed was extended in 1849 'with sliding Shutters on the South side and Iron Gates'.

35 The Sugar Tongue, showing shed with slate roof.

It was found, however, that the Old Tongue was in urgent need of repairs. It, the Lime Tongue and the Bulwark were all tending to lean and sink towards the Harbour. Dredging operations were seriously undermining the foundations of the several piers, with dramatic results. To remedy the problem, metal tie rods were inserted into the piers in order to strengthen them, 'as the least expense in these times of depression in the Harbour Funds'. Eventually very expensive work had to be undertaken to underpin the foundations. It was also reported at the same time that the Sugar Tongue needed 'an early replacement of the centre part most exposed to the action of the Horse Feet and Cart Wheels, using Granite or White Freestone to be had near Tom Herd's Rock'.

Also, the Trustees periodically carried out exercises in the reduction of staffing levels, in order to reduce expenditure. In 1849, the Harbour Master's staff had grown to one foreman, two joiners, two masons, three labourers and one privy keeper: a total wage bill of £377 per year. One joiner, one mason and one labourer were dismissed and the wages of most of the others reduced, to effect a saving of £150 per year. The privy keeper, incidentally, who had been paid 5s. per week, was reduced to 4s. Six months later, on appeal, his shilling was reinstated!

During the 1870s and 1880s, Queen's Dock and the Sea Walls between Custom House Quay and the Bulwark were built and, apart from extensive repairs to the Lime Tongue in 1881, no other major work was found necessary. Consequently, at the time of the hand over to the Harbour Commissioners in 1894, the Harbour was in good structural order.

Deepening and Cleaning the Harbour

Keeping the Harbour clean and to the correct depth was a continuous and difficult problem. Many thousand tons of mud and sand had to be removed regularly, particularly from the South and North Harbours, in order to prevent silting up. Over many years this task was undertaken simply by men digging out the silt at low tide.

However, in 1848 the Trustees decided to buy a steam dredger. It was built by the Neath Abbey Company, and was towed from there to Whitehaven, arriving in November 1848. The arrangements for the tow were made by Mr. Nicholson, the Harbour Master, who received a gratuity of £10 for his services. The original cost of the machine was £6,000, the insurance premium while under tow was £132 16s. 1d., and the fee for towing, paid to the Defiance Steam Co., was £310. The dredger was put to work immediately, and by the following August had lifted 34,385 tons of mud and sand from the bed of the Harbour at a cost of £1,133, or 7.9d. per ton. But it was calculated that the work could have been done using hand labour, and the silt carried out to sea in the hoppers, for as little as 6d. per ton. As the South and North Harbours had been deepened as far as it was prudent to go, and as the machine could not be fully employed in the Outer Harbour alone, it was decided, therefore, that the boilers and engine be cleaned and the dredger laid up. The Trustees agreed that they should not have bought it! A request from Holyhead for the hire of the dredger was turned down, but later it was allowed to go to work at Barrow.

By 1878, the Trustees were themselves hiring dredgers from other harbours. In that year, Messrs York were dredging under contract, while in 1888 the Trustees had a machine on hire from Workington. The same year Messrs W.N. Smith were contracted to remove 10,000 tons of sand from the Outer Harbour at 1s. 3d. per ton. Throughout this period the Trustees' own dredger was still laid up.

Because of financial difficulties, it is clear that only a minimum amount of dredging was done during the last decade of the 19th century. The Harbour became badly silted up; there was no water at low tide between the outer pier heads, whereas there had been nine feet of water 60 years previously.

Ballast and the Hoppers

There are very few recorded incidents of problems over ballast during the 19th century. The system of hoppers, which carried discharged ballast out to sea, proved to be very successful. There were at least five hoppers working in the Harbour between 1800 and 1825, and they were always maintained to a high standard.

A major repair was carried out on hopper No. 5 in 1820, which required 'a new Keel, two 5" Planks on each Bilge, a Bottom Plank and a Plank of the Well, all to be of Quebec Oak, and Flooring and Futtocks, a Frame of the Well and Scarfs of Stem and Stern Posts to be made of English Oak. The vessel to be new Trenailed and put in complete and good repair'. The work was carried out by Harrison & Co. at a cost of £298. Beginning in January 1881, the hoppers were used to carry the town's refuse out to sea at a charge of 5d. per load, and this was continued for many years.

Accidents to Ships

Mostly because of bad weather, there were several accidents to ships over the years. Vessels were driven on to the rocks, collided with the piers, or foundered near the Harbour. However, there were one or two incidents involving rather unusual features.

Someone went on board the brig *Traveller*, moored at the Low Hurry in the North Harbour, during the night of 16 February 1816, and cut one of the main shrouds and lanyards. The captain and owners offered a reward of 50 guineas for information leading to the discovery of the culprit and, because of the seriousness of the offence, the Trustees offered to double the reward.

Occasionally, tricky problems had to be solved. In late 1816,

The Sloop Prosperity of Aberyswith, John Jones, Master, loaden with a cargo of Flax and Linen for Mr Birley and others was driven on shore behind the North Wall by Stress of Weather, there discharged and injured. The question is

36 Shipwreck between Whitehaven and Parton. This dramatic scene is from an engraving by W.R. Smith, based on a painting by W.M.T. Turner.

whether the Harbour Duties ought to be levied by the Collector for this Cargo, the vessel not being actually in the Harbour when the Cargo was discharged, tho' she lay within the limits as described by the Act of Parliament.

The Trustees decided 'That the Duties should not be levied under present circumstances.'

A most unfortunate accident occurred in June 1849, when the steamer *Whitehaven* was entering the Harbour. The engineer tried to jump from the ship to the pier, but he missed his footing, fell into the sea and was drowned.

After 1850, it became the practice for ship owners to use solicitors when making claims against the Trustees. In 1859, a claim was received from Messrs Brockbank and

Helder, a local firm with offices at 44 Duke Street, for £125 5s. 0d. in respect of damage to the ship *Lark* and her cargo. It appears that the matter was settled out of court, the Trustees offering half the claim.

Altercations with Ships' Masters

It was not unknown for ships' masters to try to leave the Harbour without paying the appropriate duties and charges, and some were taken to court to recover unpaid sums. This problem became more serious later in the century as adjacent ports reduced or abolished charges, and one of the harbour boatmen was paid a small retainer to keep an eye on the situation. However, this proved ineffective and, in 1855, an inspector of cargoes was appointed to 'prevent the Evasion of Harbour Dues'.

One merchant, in 1858, refused to pay the dues on a consignment of sulphuric acid, on the grounds that it was not included in the list of items on which dues were payable. After some debate, he paid the dues for oil of vitriol, which was listed!

The pier master continued to have his difficulties with ships' masters:

> The Pier Master, this day preferred a Complaint against Mr Jeffrey Hannah, Master of the John and Esther, for disobedience of orders. Mr Younger [the Trustees' solicitor] is to prosecute for the offence in conformity to existing Laws of the Harbour, and also for throwing off an end without the authority of the said Pier Master, and contrary to a Bye Law made 21 March 1763.

Hannah was fined £50 by the local magistrates but, 'as he showed extreme sorrow', and as it was his first offence, the fine was reduced to £5.

The complaints were not always levelled at the ships' masters. Occasionally, charges were made against the crew of the Harbour boat, who by all accounts must have been a rough and ill-disciplined lot. In 1815:

> I am directed by the owners of the Brig William to request a Meeting of the Trustees of the Harbour on Friday 13 October 1815, to hear a Complaint against the Crew of the Harbour Boat for negligence in attending the said vessel on her entrance into the Harbour on the Evening of Tuesday the 3rd and Morning of the 4th inst: likewise for Abusive Language given by the Seamen. Sir: Yours etc Richd Bowden, Master.

The crew were found guilty of carrying an end to the Bulwark, when Captain Bowden required it to be taken to the Old Quay, and also that they made use of improper language. They were severely reprimanded.

The maintenance of discipline, particularly among the crews of the Harbour boat and hoppers, was a recurring feature. After some trouble in 1835, the Harbour Master was given powers to dismiss any of the crew of the Harbour boat as he saw fit: 'The

Trustees will consider the whole blame will rest with him if he has any inefficient or drunken men in the employ'.

In 1840, allegations were made that the duty on iron ore was being evaded by under-declaration of the quantity loaded aboard vessels. The allegations proved to be well founded and, for the future, each ship was to be deemed to be carrying its registered tonnage plus one third; for example, a vessel of 120 tons was to be charged for 160 tons of ore.

The Treatment of Workpeople

In the days before the National Health Service and state pensions, the problems of ill health and retirement must have been a constant source of worry for employees. Although under no obligation, the Trustees were not always unsympathetic in these situations, but their generosity can only be described as erratic and inconsistent. In 1812 Richard Walker, master of one of the hoppers for the past 34 years, was granted a pension of 4s. 6d. per week on his retirement, 'for his faithful and diligent service'. However, in 1851, when Charles Ross, who had been employed on the hoppers for more than 40 years, applied for a pension at the age of 77, the Trustees resolved 'to give him some employment suitable to his age and capacity'.

The senior employees did not receive any preferential treatment, although it is only fair to point out that most of them worked part-time only for the Board, and had other sources of income. Nevertheless, Joseph Hodgson, collector, in 1851 applied for an assistant because of his ill health, and offered to pay him out of his own salary or to take a reduced salary. The Trustees decided to dismiss him and to advertise for a successor. Hodgson had been in the post for more than 30 years, but it was only after considerable argument that he was granted an ex gratia payment of £50 (six months' salary). One of Hodgson's successors fared no better: in 1872, Bewley applied for a salary increase. The application was refused, and he was told that he could always resign if he did not find the situation to his satisfaction. Bewley resigned. Some years later, Pickering, the town surveyor, also asked for an increase in salary. Pickering was advised to resign, but as he refused to do so, was given three months' notice. This man was well thought of as surveyor and, on the expiry of his notice, the Trustees gave him an honorarium of £100.

The Trustees continued their practice of paying medical bills for men injured at work. For instance, in 1856 when Alex Bowen fell into excavations at the Bulwark he was awarded £12 7s. 0d. compensation. Later in the century, however, after Workmen's Compensation Legislation had come into force, some workmen chose to sue the Board for damages. A man named Quale, injured in an accident involving a dockside crane, sued the Trustees through his solicitors Brockbank and Helder. He was awarded £70 damages.

Staff

The Harbour Master

At the beginning of the 19th century, the Harbour was operated by a pier master and an assistant. After completion of the North Harbour, a Harbour Master was appointed with two assistants, one for the South Side and one for the North. At first the assistant for North Side was paid £5 per year more than his colleague on South Side, but later the salaries were equalised at £60 p.a. The first appointee on North Side was Thomas Caile, who happened to be the licensee of a public house in the town. Employees of the Board were not allowed to be publicans, and the matter was raised several times at meetings of the Trustees. However, Caile did not give up his pub!

In 1875, an advertisement appeared for a new harbour master aged under 40 years, at a salary of £150. This resulted in the appointment of Captain Thomas Mann who had a distinguished career in the position.

The Collector of Duties

After many years during which the position was vacant, a collector of duties was again appointed in 1816. This was John Hodgson, whose son, also John, succeeded him in the office. The office continued until 1894 and the incorporation of the borough, by which time the incumbent was Captain Daniel Burnyeat.

The Secretary/Treasurer

Very little change was made to the role of the secretary/treasurer for many years. Following the passing of the Act of 1816, Robert Blakeney was appointed to the position at a salary of £125 per annum. Among his functions was that of overseeing the books of Hodgson, the collector, and of E.H. Heywood, the town's officer.

In a short time, it became apparent that necessary financial information was not always available, and that the accounts were not kept up to date. Whereas Blakeney had worked only part-time, it was decreed that his successor, Richard Whiteside, should be a full-time employee, and should have no outside interests.

Lord Lonsdale intervened in this appointment, writing that he would have preferred someone from the Customs House. He added that it was unfair on Whiteside to have to work full time as (a) there was not enough work, and (b) none of his predecessors had been so restricted. Nevertheless, the Trustees appointed Whiteside, and at a lower salary than Blakeney had enjoyed. Only two years later, a clerk joined Whiteside as his assistant and 'to see that information is made available, and that all cash discounts are taken'.

Whiteside held the position until his death in 1840, when Edwin Holwell Heywood took on the job jointly with that of town's officer. In 1848, John Musgrave, a solicitor, succeeded to the position, at which time the job title was changed to that of clerk/receiver. During his incumbency, the state of the accounts again deteriorated.

Recommendations to improve the system were made by a firm of Liverpool account-ants in 1851 and, although these were agreed to, the Trustees, ever unwilling to spend money on the accountancy function, refused to appoint the clerk necessary to imple-ment the improvements.

However, it became imperative that something be done and, in 1861, a clerk was appointed to assist the receiver and 'to be a check on monies due to the Harbour'. The appointee was William Bewley, an accountant, who until then had been collector of the lamp and paving rate. As a result of the Local Government Act 1861, the form of accounting was changed and, in order to carry out the increased work, an assistant was found for Bewley. In 1872, Bewley resigned after a difference of opinion with the Trustees about his salary, but was appointed external auditor in 1876.

The duties of the clerk/receiver do not seem to have been particularly onerous. In 1862, the office holder was required to attend on only three days each week 'from 11 am to 1 pm, in a room provided at the Town Hall'. For this he received £150 per year, and was able to follow his own profession. Musgrave resigned in 1864, and was succeeded by John Collins, also a solicitor, who was still in the post in 1894.

The Rate Collector

In 1811, the Trustees received a letter from Lord Lonsdale, instructing them to appoint his nominee, one John Howard, as collector of the lamp and paving rate. He was also to superintend the regulation of the markets, and the paving of the streets. The then rate collector, Francis Dawson, was simply told he was dismissed and was instructed to hand over his books and accounts.

Three rates were being collected in Whitehaven by the late 1860s: the lamp and paving, the water and the sewerage, and all were collected by the same individual who was paid a salary of £90 per year. However, the system in operation proved to be most inefficient. Incorrect amounts were being charged and the amount of arrears was growing alarmingly. In an attempt to remedy this situation, two rate collectors were appointed in 1874, one to collect the lamp and paving rate, and the other the water and sewerage. Shortly afterwards, John Douglas, the collector of the lamp and paving rate was found to be absent from work. His claim that he was ill proved to be false, with the consequence that he was dismissed. His accounts were found to be deficient by £258 2s. 8d.

Other Employees

As a result of the Act of 1816, a police force was started in Whitehaven. The first head constable was George Kissuck, who was also responsible for a separate force, the Harbour Police. The police continued under the control of the Trustees until the late 1850s, when responsibility was taken over by the newly formed Cumberland County Police.

37   The old water front, West Strand.

Following the death, in 1839, of David Logan, the engineer responsible for the design of the head of the West Pier, the Trustees decided to appoint the first harbour engineer under their own direction. Their choice was Ebenezer Stiven, whose work included the keeping of the piers in repair, the cleaning and deepening of the Harbour, and the supervision of the workmen employed by the Harbour Master. Later, in 1866, the job of harbour engineer was combined with that of town surveyor.

In 1855, an inspector of cargoes was appointed, to 'prevent evasion of Harbour Dues'. Towards the end of the century, the holder of this position was also made traffic manager, to supervise the traffic on the Harbour railways.

A medical officer of health, responsible to the Trustees, was first appointed in 1864, with powers to implement the provisions of the Public Health Acts. Although he reported adversely on sanitary conditions in the town, the Trustees ruled that many of his recommendations were 'impractical and not capable of being carried out'.

The full list of senior officers of the Board, at the time of the incorporation of the borough in 1894 was as follows:

Secretary/Treasurer	John Collins
Town Surveyor and Harbour Engineer	John S. Brodie AMICE
Assistant ditto	Ernest Stiven

Harbour Master	Capt. Thomas Mann
Deputy Harbour Master	William Gair
Collector of Harbour Dues	Capt. Daniel Burnyeat
Medical Officer of Health	John Fisher MB CM
Inspector of Nuisances & Markets	Robert Bertram
Collector of Rates	Thomas Allinson
Captain of Fire Brigade	William Kelly, Police Supt.
Inspector of Common Lodging Houses	James Steele, Police Sergt.
Solicitor to the Board	Thomas Brown, 12 Scotch St.

Chapter 13

Trade through Whitehaven Harbour

Exports

The Coal Trade

When Sir William Lowther inherited the Whitehaven estates in 1802, the Harbour was largely reliant for its prosperity on the export of coals. However, mainly because of the incompetence of Lowther's agent, Thomas Wylie, exports were at their lowest level for some 25 years. Lowther therefore, dismissed Wylie and re-appointed John Bateman with the task of improving both mine output and shipments of coal to restore the profitability of the mines. Following some re-organisation, Bateman succeeded in increasing shipped tonnage from 90,000 to 200,000 tons per annum between 1802 and 1810. He was dismissed, however, in rather strange circumstances in 1811, and John Peile took over as principal agent. Under his regime tonnages continued to increase, but he was helped, to some extent, by the high demand and high price for coal in Dublin during the closing years of the Napoleonic Wars.

During those wars, the traffic to Ireland was again severely disrupted, and not only by enemy action. Again, seamen were impressed into naval service by the press gangs which operated both in Whitehaven and Dublin. Shipping was also delayed as a result of the Quota Acts of 1795, under which each port and county in the United Kingdom was required to provide a specific number of recruits for the Royal Navy. Whitehaven's share of the Quota was 700 men, and ships were not allowed to leave port until the requisite number had been enlisted.

During his early years in charge, Peile encountered difficulties with recalcitrant leaders who were employed to convey coal on the waggonways from the pits to the Harbour staithes. Strikes by the leaders resulted in stockpiles of coals at the pits, but a shortage at the Harbour. Peile, therefore, in 1813 built the Howgill Inclined Plane which was designed to displace 40 men and horses. Three waggons descended the incline simultaneously, and the rope to which they were attached, working over a pulley at the head of the incline, drew up empty waggons. A device, driven by the descending waggons, forced air into a cylinder, the increasing pressure, acting as a brake. The staithes were altered in 1838 at considerable expense.

38   West Strand, the Hurries and coal chutes in 1902.

On the North Wall, coals were lowered into the ships using an ingenious hydraulic mechanism invented and built by Tulk and Ley, Lowca: 'The coals are dropped from a waggon into a box supported by an unseen rod, which, on turning a tap, is permitted to descend by forcing water from a cylinder below, into an ornamental tank placed on columns over the waggon. When the coals are let fall into the hold, the water, again descending, raises the empty box'.

After a long recession during the 1820s, Whitehaven regained its position as the first port in West Cumberland during the following decade, exporting more coals than Maryport, Workington and Harrington combined. During this period annual tonnages averaged 150-185,000 tons, and reached the high figure of 230,000 in 1845.

However, the opening of the Maryport and Carlisle Railway in the 1840s was instrumental in helping Maryport to take over as the principal supplier of coals to Ireland, and by 1875 Whitehaven had almost lost its trade to Dublin. Later, Maryport concentrated on the import and export of iron ore, pig iron, and steel rails, and Whitehaven was able to regain some of the lost ground. Although large quantities of coal continued to be produced from Whitehaven's pits, an ever decreasing proportion was being shipped through the Harbour. Annual tonnages remained similar to those of 1810, a situation which exacerbated the declining fortunes of the Harbour. By 1900, up to 30 per cent of mine output was being carried by rail for use in the furnaces of the iron and steel industries at Workington and Millom, and, of course, coals were taken to many other parts of the country, also by rail.

Throughout the 19th century, coal shipments were the mainstay of the economic life of Whitehaven Harbour. Of course, there were periods of slump and boom as demand and prices varied but, after 1860, Whitehaven began to decline as adjacent ports equipped with better rail access and wet docks increased their share of the trade to Ireland, the market on which Whitehaven so heavily depended. However, by the end of the century, the Irish market was dominated by coals from the Scottish and Lancashire coalfields which were able to dump their surpluses in Ireland.

39   South Harbour with the Hurries.

Iron Ore

Sufficient iron ore was being shipped through Whitehaven Harbour by 1700 to warrant the erection of a small staithe near the end of the Old Pier. The ore was mined in the Egremont area and brought to the Harbour on packhorses, but the quantities cannot have been significant as the 'old iron ore staithe' was removed in 1733 to make way for the new coal staithes.

Small tonnages continued to be exported over the years, but it was not until 1841, and the establishment of the Whitehaven Hematite Iron Company at Cleator Moor, that the mining of iron ore in the area began in earnest. Much of the ore was used by the Cleator Moor company, but Thomas Ainsworth, one of the founding partners, sent many thousands of tons of ore via the Whitehaven, Cleator and Egremont Railway and the Market Place Tramway to the Harbour for onward shipment in his own vessels. His principal market was South Wales, but he and others also sent many large cargoes to Scotland and Shropshire. *Slater's Directory*, of 1894, tells us that, although shipments at that time had almost ceased, at their peak up to 330,000 tons of ore were exported annually through the port.

The introduction of the railways enabled the owners of the iron and steel industries to build their plant remote from the source of the ore, and many furnaces were erected at Workington and Maryport. The necessary ore was at first transported along the coast railway through Whitehaven Tunnel, but after 1863 it was carried over the Whitehaven, Cleator and Egremont Railway Extension via Marron Junction, and after 1879 over the newly-built Cleator and Workington Junction Railway.

Consumption of iron ore by the local iron and steel manufacturers increased dramatically, and soon there was little surplus for export. From about the mid-1870s shipped tonnages through Whitehaven began to decrease, and ceased completely in 1896. At that date Cumberland iron ore production was about 1.25 million tons per annum, but it was all transported away from the immediate area by rail. In fact, during the last 30 years of the century, cheaper ore was brought in from Spain but, of the three million tons imported between 1880 and 1890, Whitehaven received only 83,000 tons, a tiny fraction of the total. Again, Workington and particularly Maryport were much better placed.

The shipment of major quantities of iron ore through Whitehaven Harbour was comparatively short lived, but nevertheless was of great importance as, for a short period, exported tonnages exceeded those of coal.

Other Exports

The *Parson and White Directory* (1829) notes that 'Whitehaven does not appear to be in a state of retrogradation, for besides the coal trade to Ireland etc, its commerce is now extended to Africa, America, the West Indies, and the principal ports in Europe'. Goods manufactured in the immediate vicinity of the town included linen, sail-cloth, checks, damask and diaper, cabinet goods, earthernware, colours, copperas, ropes, snuff tobacco, soap, candles, anchors, cables, nails, etc. Besides coal and iron ore, large quantities of lime were shipped for Scotland from the Lime Tongue. Exported quantities of these goods were always small; Whitehaven never established a substantial manufacturing base, and trade was mainly limited to Ireland, the Isle of Man, and other ports around the coast of England, particularly Liverpool.

The *Mannex and Whelan Directory* (1847) states that in addition to the goods mentioned, excellent pig iron from the Whitehaven Hematite Iron Works at Cleator Moor was shipped for Liverpool, London and other places. During the final decade of the century, the list of exported goods included stone, alabaster, steel rails and sleepers.

Imports

Tobacco continued to be imported into Whitehaven until well into the 19th century. In 1829, the annual quantity was approximately 5,000 hogsheads, 'Glasgow having stolen that branch'. This level of imports was only about a quarter of the former record levels.

The principal imports throughout the period were grain and timber from America, Canada and the Baltic, fruit from the Mediterranean, wine from Portugal and Spain, and large quantities of flax, linen and other goods from Ireland. The 1829 *Directory* shows four Whitehaven merchants trading with the West Indies, one with the East Indies, one with the Mediterranean, and three trading in flax and linen. The West Indies merchants brought in large quantities of sugar—hence the name of the Sugar Tongue. There were also wines and spirits merchants importing wines from Spain and Portugal, and rum from the West Indies. By 1847, the number of overseas merchants had been reduced to four, two of whom imported sugar. There were also seven merchants engaged in the importation of wines and spirits.

The number of ships belonging to Whitehaven in 1828 was 197, reduced from 216 in 1790. The total tonnage was 30,960, showing that the ships of the time were amazingly small, having an average burthen of only 160 tons. Twenty years or so later, there were 267 vessels registered at Whitehaven with an aggregate tonnage of 42,000, or a little below 160 tons on average. The number of men working on these vessels amounted to some 2,250. The ships visiting Whitehaven for most of the century were small, the average burthen being consistently below 200 tons.

It is noticeable that although there continued to be a considerable number of ships registered at Whitehaven, some, never even visited the Harbour and, increasingly, the masters and crews were found elsewhere. Part of the problem was the level of dues and charges levied on ships and goods passing through the Harbour. At a meeting in 1867, several of Whitehaven's traders were invited by the Trustees to give their comments. One vessel, the *Hardware* registered tonnage 147 tons, was engaged in the iron ore trade and was charged:

Tonnage dues		2 15	10
60 tons ballast @ 6d		1 10	0
Lamps		3	1
245 tons Iron Ore duty		13	7
	£5	2	6

The tonnage dues included one halfpenny per registered ton for the use of the steam tug, the lamp rate was at one farthing per registered ton, while the ore duty was calculated at two-thirds of a penny per ton loaded. The total added 5d. per ton to the cost of the iron ore.

An importer engaged in the Irish trade brought in from Dublin a cargo which included butter, rags, hides, bacon, feathers, porter, eggs, lard and fat cattle, but he had the vessel routed via Workington, claiming that the amount of the duties through Whitehaven exceeded the cost of the rail carriage from Workington to Whitehaven.

Passenger Traffic

Throughout the 19th century, regular passenger services were operated by sea from Whitehaven. In 1829, for instance, the traveller 'goes on board the (steam) packet in the evening, where he can, in moderate weather, sleep as comfortably in his own bed, and be landed at Liverpool in the morning, ready to proceed on his business, paying only 15 shillings for the accommodation'. At the time, the journey from Whitehaven to Liverpool took two entire days by stage coach, and was very expensive.

The tourist could also obtain steam conveyances by the *St Andrew* to Douglas and Dublin every Thursday evening, to Dumfries every Monday and Thursday morning, returning the same days. The service to Liverpool was by the *Countess of Lonsdale* every Monday and Thursday, whence she returned every Monday and Wednesday morning. There was also a service to Wigtown and Kirkcudbright every alternate Wednesday, returning the same day.

The *St Andrew* and the *Countess of Lonsdale* were paddle steamers owned and operated by the Whitehaven Steam Navigation Company. In 1847, the Whitehaven Steam Navigation Company's vessels operated between Whitehaven and Liverpool three times per week during the summer months and twice per week in the winter months. A service between Whitehaven and Belfast was operated twice per week in summer, but only once each week in winter. There was also a weekly steamer between Whitehaven, the Isle of Man and Dublin during the summer months only.

In 1885, there were plans to start a daily service between Whitehaven and the Isle of Man, but they were abandoned in 1888, possibly because the Trustees insisted that the vessels moor at the West Pier, instead of at the Sugar Tongue as did all the other steamers. In addition, the Cumberland Steam Packet Company ran a weekly service between Carlisle and Liverpool, calling at Whitehaven for passengers.

In 1894, there were still extensive passenger sailings from Whitehaven, despite the railway alternative. The *Minnie Hinde* sailed to Belfast every Tuesday, Thursday and Saturday, returning on Monday, Wednesday and Friday. A service to Dundrum by the *Lady Arthur Hill* sailed 'regularly'. Dublin was served by the steamships *Thistle*, *Adela* and *Magnet*, one of which sailed every Thursday and returned on Saturday. The service to Ramsay was only once per fortnight, but the Dublin, Silloth and Isle of Man steamers sailed three times per week to Douglas and Dublin. There was also a twice weekly service to Liverpool by the *Margaret*, a vessel owned by Pattinson and Winter who built the corn mills on North Shore. At this time the Carlisle to Liverpool service had been discontinued, and the owners refused to recommence sailings as it was 'inconvenient'.

Chapter 14

Steam Tugs, Lifeboats and Fortifications

Steam Tugs

Early in 1839, Henry Jefferson proposed that a steam tug should be purchased to tow ships in and out of the Harbour, in order to replace the arduous work previously carried out by rowing boats manned from the ships' crew. Obviously, charges would be made for the use of the tug, thereby generating revenue. However, the Trustees decided that, with their existing powers, they were unable to own such a vessel. Jefferson, therefore, along with Richard Barker and others, undertook to form a company to buy and operate a steam tug in the Harbour, with the proviso that the vessel would not be liable to Harbour dues and charges.

A tug, the *Prince Albert*, a paddle steamer, was put into service in 1840. At first it was not particularly successful, as the ships' masters, objecting to the charges, continued with the old methods. Indeed, it is noticeable that many of those most in favour of the tug in the initial stages were amongst those most reluctant to use it. As a result the tug company failed, and the *Prince Albert* was handed over to the Trustees, who were convinced of the potential viability of a tug service. The minutes of the Board of Trustees disclose that, in September 1848, the master of the tug was dismissed for misconduct and neglect of duty. The very next minute states that 'the damage recently sustained by Prince Albert' was repaired by Tulk and Ley, Lowca, at a cost of £154 11s. 3d.

By 1851, *Prince Albert* was an established feature of operations in Whitehaven Harbour, and when, in that year, the vessel required refurbishment, a steam vessel, the *Earl of Lonsdale*, was leased from Whitehaven Steam Navigation for £60 per week, pending the return of the tug to service. Indeed, the tug had become almost indispensable, and whenever *Prince Albert* was out of service, a suitable vessel, such as the *Prince of Wales* from Annan, or the *Lady Charlotte* from Dublin, was always hired to replace her. In fact, the tug had become so popular by 1854, that the Trustees decided to buy a second vessel. This was the *Ajax*, bought in London for £1,350, and already 20 years old. She was sailed around the coast, and on arrival at Whitehaven she was registered in the name of the secretary to the Trustees. This vessel came into service in October 1858. At about this time, the charge for towing a vessel out to sea was £19. There were

148

40 *Prince of Wales* paddle tug at the Sugar Tongue in 1905.

instances, however, when the charge was not levied in full, as in the case of the brig *Richardson*, which was lost off St Bees Head immediately after being towed out. The charge, in this instance, was reduced to £10.

In service, *Ajax* was found to be seriously underpowered, and in 1861 the decision was taken to commission a custom-built tug of 100/110 HP from C & W Earle of Hull. This vessel arrived at Whitehaven in November 1862 and was registered as the *Prince of Wales*.

After almost 30 years in service, it was found that *Prince Albert* required very extensive repairs, in fact almost a rebuild. The cost was prohibitive, so she was sold by public auction on 7 July 1868 for £170. A replacement tug was then ordered from the Whitehaven Shipbuilding Company, with a delivery date of 29 June 1875. When the day arrived, the new tug was ready but could not be delivered as the Trustees were unable to pay for her. After some negotiation with the directors of the Shipbuilding Company, the tug was released, still not paid for, in October 1875. She entered service named *Whitehaven*. This vessel, although successful, had a very short life, as she was lost most unfortunately off the Isle of Man in June 1879. This was a severe blow to the Trustees, as *Whitehaven* was not insured, and a loss of over £10,000 was sustained.

Before the completion of the water supply, fresh water for the tug's boiler was brought at considerable expense, usually from Bransty Gill. Later, the tugs were supplied from the mains and, on the insistence of the Water Committee, the Harbour was charged £12 per tug per annum.

Throughout their working careers, the Whitehaven steam tugs earned useful revenue by carrying passengers, principally on holiday trips. *Prince Albert* for several years operated between Fleetwood and Piel (near Barrow) carrying day trippers, and *Whitehaven* worked between Whitehaven and the Isle of Man. On these trips, *Whitehaven* had stewardesses, and even had a liquor licence. The tugs, all paddle steamers, were powerful vessels, capable of towing several ships simultaneously. However, accidents occasionally happened. In November 1848, *Prince of Wales* was towing out three schooners, the *Enterprise*, the *William and Sarah*, and the *Splendid*, together with one of the Harbour hoppers. At the entrance to the Harbour, the tug lost steerage way, and all three schooners came into contact with the West Pier. The owners of the ships sued the Trustees for the cost of repairs, but the extent of the damage was only slight. The bill for *Enterprise* was £9 10s. 0d., for *William and Sarah*, £3 15s. 0d. and for *Splendid*, £6 15s. 0d.

What ultimately happened to *Ajax* is not clear, but *Prince of Wales* was still in use in 1880, as she was reboiled in that year by Fletcher Jennings (formerly Tulk and Ley), Lowca, even though the firm submitted the highest of the four tenders received. Shortly after this, *Prince of Wales* disappeared from the records. During the 1880s and 1890s the port of Whitehaven was in sad decline, and it seems that the Trustees merely hired tugs as they were needed. For instance in 1893 alone, the *Senhouse* was hired from Maryport, and the *Dunrobin*, *Refuge* and *Florence* from Dublin.

Lifeboats

Many accidents happened to ships along the coast of west Cumberland, putting at risk the lives of the crew. Until the 19th century, there were few aids to navigation, and almost no facilities for the rescue of ships in distress.

Following a series of accidents near Whitehaven in the 1790s, the Trustees decided to provide a lifeboat. The first boat was 'the largest size Lifeboat' built by Henry Greathead at South Shields. It was transported overland with great difficulty and at enormous cost, and arrived in October or November 1803 in Whitehaven where it was housed on the North Shore outside the North Wall. It was put to its greatest test in 1813.

> 18 November 1813—During the violent Storm of yesterday, the Brig *Brothers* of Workington, George Sparke, Master, laden with Cattle from Bangor in Ireland, appeared off this port in the greatest distress and soon afterwards came on Shore near the Entrance of the Harbour. To aid her, and to endeavour to save the Crew, the Harbour Boat was voluntarily manned by five persons, one of whom, Thomas Farell, perished in the humane attempt to save his fellow creatures. The remainder of the Boats Crew were rescued by the Exertions of numerous Individuals, and the Ships Crew saved by the same Means with the Assistance of the Lifeboat.

It is therefore recommended that a sum not exceeding Thirty Guineas be advanced by the Trustees of the Harbour out of the Harbour Funds, to Messrs Steward, Birkett and Fisher for them to discriminate and reward each individual who distinguished himself on that Melancholy Occasion.

It is further recommended that the situation of the Lifeboat shall in future be so placed as to be ready upon every emergency for immediate use, and that Mr Peile, assisted by Messrs Jefferson, Steward and Birkett, do fix upon the most Eligible Place for its ultimate Destination.

A copy of this minute was sent to Lord Lonsdale, who replied sending 'a private consideration of my own'.

Obviously, the rescue was not an overwhelming success. The lifeboat was considered to be too big and clumsy, while attempts to launch from the North Shore directly into the teeth of the gale had proved extremely difficult. A new lifeboat house, designed by John Peile, was built on the shore between the Old and New Piers: 'a Situation affording the greatest facility for the Boat to be got into the Water'. The boat was moved there in 1814.

Five years later, John Peile and Henry Birley were detailed to obtain a new lifeboat, 'smaller than the one in use'. Again, the Trustees chose to go to the north east, an area which had, apparently, a reputation for building lifeboats. Indeed, a deputation of Trustees travelled over 'to inspect the construction of the Lifeboat'. It seems strange that a suitable boat could not be found at Whitehaven, a place with a first-class reputation for building ships and boats for all purposes. Perhaps this thought encouraged Thomas Cowan, in 1823, to build a boat which he offered to the Trustees as a lifeboat for £60. Unfortunately, it is not recorded whether Cowan's offer was accepted.

From the beginning, the lifeboat had been manned by volunteers, but on an ad hoc basis. The situation was changed in 1858, with the establishment of a regular lifeboat crew. In 1864, the RNLI offered to take over the lifeboat, but the Trustees refused. However, the boat was moved back to its original station outside the North Wall. The following year, the Trustees were given a new lifeboat, which was named *Elizabeth*. The lifeboat, the lifeboat house and all ancillary apparatus were handed over to the RNLI on 13 December 1869. The Trustees also promised to make an annual donation to the Institution of £10.

Several devices ancillary to sea rescue were tried out over the years. Thus a letter to Lord Lonsdale regarding 'the inefficiency of Manby's Life Preserver under Lieut. Dunderdale'. It is a pity that the Trustees did not make clear which was at fault, the life preserver or the Lieutenant! Later, Donnett's 'Apparatus for the Safety of Life and Property in Cases of Shipwreck' was purchased for the sum of £29 2s. 6d. Six 'Patent Rockets and a Rocket Line' were obtained in 1849. A rocket brigade was formed which, although continuing to operate from Whitehaven, was handed over to the coastguard

41   Practice launch of Whitehaven lifeboat, *c.*1910.

for operational purposes in 1864. In 1891, the Board of Trade proposed moving the rocket brigade to St Bees. The Trustees, of course, made a strong protest, and after some discussion, the brigade was allowed to stay at Whitehaven provided that a force of 25 men was trained to the required standard, maintained and made available at all times.

The Fortifications

The defences of Whitehaven remained virtually unchanged throughout the duration of the Napoleonic Wars. The guns in the Fort, Halfmoon Battery, the Bowling Green, Jack a Dandy and Redness Point were kept in readiness by men from the Invalid Battalion of the Royal Artillery. After so many years of war the British Government began to demobilise most of the armed forces as an economy measure and, as part of this process, the Board of Ordnance wrote to the Trustees:

Newcastle - 19 September 1817.

I have the honour to address you in obedience to the commands of the Board of Ordnance on the subject of dismounting the Guns on the Forts and Batteries at Whitehaven. It is the Board's constant practice in times of peace to perform this service relative to the artillery on the Works under their charge for the better preservation of their Gun Carriages, and therefore they desire me to request you to cause it to be done at Whitehaven, namely the Guns to be dismounted and skidded, and the Carriages to be placed in a Dry Store. The distance from Whitehaven of any of the Board's Troops and Officers would render it inconvenient and expensive to the public for them to attend to this business themselves, and therefore they trust you will have the Goodness to have it executed ...

Yours etc. I F Birch Lt Col. Royal Engineers.

The Trustees, of course, had built the forts at their own expense, and had also spent a great deal of money in maintaining the guns, carriages and other equipment, and were unwilling to be put to the further expense of dismantling and storage. However Lt. Col. Birch insisted that 'where defences are local, ie for the protection of the port and property, it is customary for the party particularly interested, to look after the guns and carriages'. Incidentally, Birch's last letter in this correspondence was delayed for three months, but he explained by way of apology that 'an accident happened to me at a Shooting in blowing off part of my hand'. After some consideration, the Trustees decided to leave matters as they were.

Late in 1817, it was reported that 'The sea has made a considerable Breach in the Half Moon Battery, and unless it be repaired without delay, the whole will be demolished during this Winter'. The battery was rebuilt under the supervision of John Young, the resident engineer on the Harbour works which were then being wound down.

However, 12 months later, another letter, addressed to Lord Lonsdale, arrived from the Board of Ordnance:

I beg leave to acquaint your Lordship that the Board of Ordnance have commanded me to transmit a statement of the Ordnance Stores deposited in the Storehouses at Whitehaven, pointing out such as could be withdrawn if necessary and desiring to know whether, in case it should be requisite to withdraw the Artillery Men stationed at that place, any inconvenience will result. As no account of these Stores are [sic] in the Office for my guidance, and not conceiving myself competent to give an opinion respecting the Men, I have presumed to enclose a Copy of the Board's Letter for your Information, and request your Lordship will be pleased to cause a Return of the Stores to be sent to me with your Lordship's decision respecting the Artillery Men.

The list of stores include the following:-

Iron Ordnance

42 Pounders	10 serviceable	dismounted on skids
32 Pounders	8 serviceable	dismounted on skids

| 24 Pounders | 8 serviceable | mounted in the Fort |
| 18 Pounders | 10 serviceable | dismounted on skids |

Included amongst other equipment in the list are such items as:

Spunges [sic] with Staves and Rammer Heads - 15 each for the 42's and 18's,
    and 12 each for the 32's and 24's.
Copper Gunpowder Measures for the Different Guns - 20.
Gunpowder in Barrels, Round Grain - 5,741 pounds.
Powder Horns - 12
Lanthorns - 2 Muscovy, 3 Tin and 3 Black.

Several thousand rounds of shot and grapeshot are also detailed.

In a letter of 13 October 1818 enclosing the list of stores, the Trustees wrote 'upon a due consultation on the subject, the Trustees are anxious to retain all the Stores now in their possession ... but with regard to the Invalid Artillery Men, they are perfectly indifferent ...'. The stores remained at Whitehaven, and the artillery men were withdrawn.

The authorities, however, were determined to remove the guns from Whitehaven for, in December 1819, instructions were received to send all the guns and stores to Plymouth, as 'there is insufficient protection for them at Whitehaven'. John Peile asked Lord Lonsdale for his assistance with the Board of Ordnance, commenting that 'supposing all the heavy Ordnance to be removed, this Town would be without a single gun, and be deprived of the means of showing their Loyalty, and of joining in any general Rejoicing of the Nation'.

Following Lonsdale's intervention, it was agreed that the guns in the Fort and in the Halfmoon Battery could be retained, but that all other guns and stores were to be shipped to Plymouth. Peile assessed that the shipping costs would be between 18s. and 20s. per ton for the 90-100 tons of equipment involved, in addition to £20-30 to the Harbour for collecting the guns. Some difficulty was expected with the three 42-pounders at Redness Point, as they had to be transported some distance over a soft field. After some debate as to who was to pay the necessary expenses, the stores were shipped as ordered, at the expense of the Harbour. The guns in the Fort and the Halfmoon Battery were kept for ceremonial occasions, and it seems that these guns were last fired on the occasion of the laying of the foundation stone of the new West Pier in 1824. Apparently, the remaining guns were removed in about 1830 because of the state of political unrest in the country. According to *Mannex and Whellan* in 1847, only one battery remained, but 'even that has been rendered useless'.

The idea of the undefended Harbour of Whitehaven cannot have appealed to the Board of Ordnance for, in 1855, the Trustees received the news that it was proposed to build batteries on the heads of both the West and North Piers 'for the defence of the Harbour'. The supposed danger must have receded, because nothing came of this plan. Peile and Nicholson's *Directory of Whitehaven* (1864), commenting on the fortifications, contains the note, 'The only battery now, however, belonging to the Town is the one recently constructed for the use of Artillery Volunteers, on the hill above Wellington Pit'. A huge landslip in 1872 brought thousands of tons of rock down on to the site of the Halfmoon Battery, but the guns above remained in position. There were guns on the Sea Brows site until the First World War, when they were removed.

Chapter 15

John Peile, 1776-1855

John Peile's grandfather was Thomas Peile, born in 1707 at Dean near Cockermouth. The son of a small yeoman farmer, Thomas in 1742 married Elizabeth Hotblack, daughter of the Rev. Hotblack, schoolteacher of Dean. Their second son, also Thomas, was born in 1744, and at the age of 26 he married Grace Scott, who was 20, on 29 April 1770. Thomas and Grace moved to Whitehaven *c.*1771/2 'where they set up some leather business in the town'. They had 15 children, most of whom were born in Whitehaven; the youngest was born in 1800 when Grace was 50 years of age, and the eldest child twenty-nine. After some years Thomas and Grace 'were enabled to take and carry on a brewery at Corkickle'. Their eldest son William was apprenticed to shipbuilding, and in later life he built ships on his own account at Harrington. Their 11th child, Adam Scott, took over the brewery at Corkickle when his father died in 1812. Thomas was 68 years of age and was buried in St Nicholas' churchyard. Grace Peile died in 1827 aged 77, and was also buried at St Nicholas'.

The fourth child of Thomas and Grace was John, born in 1776 at Whitehaven. His godfather was Richard Wordsworth, uncle of the poet, an attorney from Braithwaite. As a boy, John was taught to be observant and a 'ready reckoner' and, like his brothers, he went to Mr. Wood's school in Whitehaven where special attention was paid to writing and mental arithmetic.

In January 1806, at the age of 29, John married Betsy Williamson, daughter of Isaac Williamson, the principal surgeon of Whitehaven. They had four children:

Thomas—born 1807. Thomas went to school at Snittlegarth and for two years to St Bees Grammar School. He took Holy Orders and eventually became DD and headmaster of Repton public school. He married Mary Braithwaite, daughter of John Peile's second wife.

John—born 1808. John went to sea and became a Master Mariner. He died in 1848, aged forty.

Ann—born 1809. Ann died in 1813, aged four years.

Williamson—born 1810, his mother Betsy dying shortly after the birth. He was educated at St Bees Grammar School, and later began work in colliery engineering under his father in the employment of Lord Lonsdale. He also worked a mine on his own account at Gilcrux. Williamson died in 1842 aged 32 at Hastings. His wife, Lizzie, died in 1884 at Corkickle.

In 1814, at the age of 38, John married his second wife, Elizabeth Braithwaite, widow of James Braithwaite of Distington. Mrs. Braithwaite brought to the marriage a small landed estate at Distington, which John added to property he had already acquired there. She also had a daughter, Mary, who married John's eldest son Thomas Williamson. There were no children of the marriage of John and Elizabeth, and she died in 1850 and was buried at St James', Whitehaven.

John Peile began his working life in 1793 when, at the age of 16, he was placed in Lord Lonsdale's colliery office. 'Being a man of active habits and great energy and perseverence, he soon attained distinction in his situation, and ultimately succeeded to his Lordship's extensive collieries in the neighbourhood.' In 1811, at the age of 34, he was made head manager of the Lonsdale Collieries and principal agent to the Earl of Lonsdale in Whitehaven, positions which he held for 37 years until his retirement in 1848.

Among his achievements in the coal mines were:

The extension of Croft, Saltom, Duke and James pits by deepening the shafts to gain access to lower seams of coal.

The sinking of new pits—Countess, Wreay, and his greatest achievement, Wellington.

42 Wellington Pit—John Peile's greatest achievement.

The construction, in 1814, of the Howgill Surface Incline to the Howgill Staithe in the Harbour.

The initiation of the Parton Drifts, intended to drain the land and to give access to coal hitherto unobtainable. The drifts were one and a half miles long, and although not totally successful, this endeavour is regarded as one of the greatest achievements in Whitehaven mining history.

The introduction of screens to the mines.

The beginning of the manufacture of coke and patent fuel. These failed because of lack of demand.

The first trials of a steam locomotive in the area. A locomotive built to William Chapman's patent was ordered in 1816 by Peile from Phineas Crowther of the Ouseburn Foundry, Newcastle. Parts of this engine were built at Whitehaven under the supervision of Taylor Swainson, the colliery engineer. The engine was tested on the Croft Pit waggonway, where apparently it performed very well, but unfortunately the cast-iron rails were incapable of bearing its weight.

In 1816, the Whitehaven pits employed 900 people and, during his tenure of office, Peile doubled the output of coal, achieving 250,000 tons a year. He was patron of the Whitehaven Coal Miners Benevolent Society and of the Whitehaven Coal Miners Friendly Society, attending and speaking at their functions.

Peile was a Trustee of the Town and Harbour of Whitehaven from 1811 to 1850, the last three years of which he was chairman. During these 40 years he acted as Lord Lonsdale's deputy in those matters which required the presence of Lonsdale or his deputy. As a Trustee he was responsible for the supervision, on behalf of the Trustees, of much of the work carried out in the Harbour area, for example, the North Wall from the North Coin to William Pit. For these services he received several gratuitous payments from the Trustees, and was invited to lay the foundation stone of the New West Pier on 29 May 1824. He was also responsible for the supervision of the Market Hall (designed by Smirke 1814), a new lifeboat house and a small octagonal lockup in the market place (1816). During his period of office, the Trustees introduced a police force, gas lighting, street paving, and the waterworks, and Peile served personally on the several committees.

In addition to his position as Trustee of the Town and Harbour of Whitehaven, he was also a Trustee of the Whitehaven Turnpike Trust; a member of the local Board of Health; a magistrate—Justice of the Peace; a Guardian of the Poor Law Union, and Treasurer of Whitehaven Infirmary from its inception until his retirement. During the Napoleonic Wars he was a member of the local Volunteers.

For upwards of half a century, Mr. Peile took a prominent part in all public matters connected with this Port, evincing on all occasions an ardent desire to benefit and improve his native Town, and to whom perhaps Whitehaven is more indebted for the great improvements which have been effected within that period than to any other individual. In Lowther Street, the erection of both the Joint Stock Bank and the Bank for Savings originated with Peile, while he was also responsible for the handsome design of the principal room of the Public Library.

John Peile also had several business interests: he was a promoter and director of both the railways (WJR and W&FJR) into Whitehaven; he was a promoter and director of the Steam Packet companies; he was a partner in the shipbuilding firm Lumley Kennedy and Company; and was a partner and later president of the Whitehaven Joint Stock Bank.

On his retirement as Lord Lonsdale's agent a special performance was given at the Whitehaven Theatre on 26 January 1848: 'The performance at the Theatre is a bespeak on the part of the Miners of Whitehaven for Mr Peile to express their high sense of esteem and respect'. It was reported a great success. The miners also presented him with a silver cup and silver salver with an engraving of Wellington Pit. The salver, made in Edinburgh by Robb and Whittet, weighed 55 ounces, and was obtained from Edgards, Jewellers, Whitehaven. His friends in the area contributed to the handsome testimonial of a silver epergne and other articles to the value of £350, which included a legacy of £200 left by the late Earl of Lonsdale in 1844 for the purpose. The plate was presented to Peile on 23 May 1848 at a dinner held in the *Black Lion Hotel*.

John Peile was 72 years of age when he retired from Lonsdale's employment, and he spent his last years as chairman of the Board of Trustees, in attending board meetings of those companies of which he was a director, and also sitting on the bench of magistrates. He took a great interest in the shipbuilding yard at Whitehaven 'where he visited within a week of his death'. Unfortunately, his fellow Trustees did not see fit to mention his retirement as chairman in 1850, and his leaving went unremarked in the minutes.

Peile was a Tory in the Lowther interest all his life, but 'he respected his opponents, and was ever ready the day after the battle to meet with them with the full cordiality and candour of his nature'.

In private life, 'Peile was as exemplary a character as in public he was valuable. As a husband and father he was affectionate and indulgent, and to the domestics around him his kindness was proverbial'.

As a young man, he had lived with his parents firstly in Tangier Street, and later at Corkickle brewery. In 1811, he moved into Somerset House, which contained the colliery office, and lived there until 1848 when, on his retirement, he moved to 1 Lowther

Street, another house which he owned. He had a farm at Stubsgill, in which he took a great interest, and where he reared remarkably fine pigs. In 1840, he bought Prospect House, Distington, intending it to be his retirement home. However, he never lived there, mainly because his wife Elizabeth did not wish to leave Whitehaven. The house was sold after his death to Charles Fisher.

The death of John Peile was announced in the *Cumberland Pacquet* of 23 January 1855: 'One of Her Majesty's Justices of the Peace, at his house in Lowther Street on Wednesday last [17 January] at the advanced age of seventy nine years'. He was buried in the family vault at St James' church, Whitehaven.

Sources

The Minute Books of the Board of Trustees of the Town and Harbour of Whitehaven, 1802-94.

The Acts of Parliament:

       1806 - 46 Geo 3

       1816 - 56 Geo 3

       1818 - 58 Geo 3

       1858 - Whitehaven Harbour Act - 21 Vict.

       1859 - Whitehaven Town and Harbour Act - 22 Vict.

       1871 - Whitehaven Dock and Railways Act 34 & 35 Vict.

       1876 - Whitehaven Harbour and Town Improvement Act - 39 & 40 Vict.

       1879 - Whitehaven Town and Harbour Act - 42 & 43 Vict.

       1882 - Whitehaven Harbour and Dock Act - 45 & 46 Vict.

       1885 - Whitehaven Town and Harbour (Incorporation) Act - 48 & 49 Vict.

Local newspapers, especially the *Cumberland Pacquet.*

Fancy, H., *Whitehaven in Old Photographs* (1992).

Hay, D., *An Illustrated History of Whitehaven* (1979).

Hudleston, G., *Whitehaven Harbour Works during the last Century* (1904).

Jollie and Sons, *Jollie's Cumberland Guide and Directory* (1811).

Joy, D., *A Regional History of the Railways of Great Britain, Vol. 14: The Lakes Counties* (1983).

Lancaster, J.Y. and Wattleworth, D.R., *The Iron and Steel Industry of West Cumberland* (1977).

Lavery, B., *Nelson's Navy* (1989).

Mannex and Whellan, *Gazetteer and History of Cumberland* (1847).

Moore, R.W., *Historical Sketch of the Whitehaven Collieries* (1905).

Owen, C.H.H., *The Lowther Family* (1990).

Parson, William and White, William, History, *Gazetteer and Directory of the Counties of Cumberland and Westmorland* (1829).

Peile and Nicholson, *A Directory of Whitehaven* (1864).

Poll Book of the Election of a Representative in Parliament for the Borough of Whitehaven (1832).

Wood, O., *West Cumberland Coal 1600-1982/3* (1988).

Woodward, Sir Llewellyn, *The Age of Reform 1815-1870* (1962).

Part Three

The 20th Century

Chapter 16

The 20th Century

The Harbour

43 A view of Whitehaven Harbour. St James' church is on the left; Pattinson's Beacon Mills is on the right.

All the property which had been acquired over the years was vested in the Harbour Trust and, in 1894, at the time of the Incorporation of the Borough, it had to be divided and handed over, as appropriate, to the new town council, or the new Harbour Commission. It was found that the bulk of the properties was in the name of the Harbour, as Harbour funds had been used to make the original purchase. For instance, the Town Hall was Harbour property, as were several houses and coal depots scattered around the town. Included in the list of property transferred to the Harbour Commission were the Harbour itself with docks, piers, and railways, the swing bridge, the harbour offices, the Rocket Brigade House on the Old New Quay, the Bransty Isolation Hospital, the Tobacco Pipes on Bransty, and the Gunpowder Magazine, also on Bransty. The Commission began at an early stage to dispose of properties which were not directly part of the Harbour. The hospital on Bransty was disposed of for £175, while the Town Hall was rented to Whitehaven Corporation for £125 per annum. In June 1895 the Commissioners sold the Town Hall to the Council for £4,500.

The Harbour consisted of the West Pier, which had a circular lighthouse with a white light revolving every two minutes, with three reflectors and a fog horn. The Old New Quay had a house and the Rocket Brigade House on it. The Old Quay also had a house on it and two watch houses, and carried a fixed red light when there was nine feet of water at the end of the pier. Next was the Sugar Tongue. This structure was 570 feet in length by 52 feet in breadth, and was covered with a substantial slate roof supported on cast-iron columns. The shed had iron gates, was well lit by electric light, and had a good supply of water. It was also fitted with two lines of railway track, and had five two-ton hand cranes, an overhead travelling crane, and portable steam and hand

cranes to facilitate the loading and unloading of cargoes. The Lime Tongue was 600 feet long and 27 feet in breadth. There were no railway lines and the tongue was unlit. Queen's Dock, the wet dock, was 550 feet by 320 feet, covering an area of four and three-quarter acres. The length of quay was 1,530 feet, and there were railway lines on all four sides. The wet dock was also well lit by electric light and had an adequate supply of water. Last was the North Pier, which carried a fixed green light in its circular lighthouse. In addition there were railway lines along West Strand underneath the hurries and on to the West Pier. There were also several storage sheds and workshops in various parts of the Harbour.

Also listed as property forming part of the transfer were dredgers, hoppers, steam cranes, and other plant and appliances. The commissioners secured the future of the hoppers by entering into a 10-year contract with the town council to dispose of all the town's refuse by carrying it out to sea. The council agreed to pay 7d. per ton. Two new 60-ton steel hoppers were purchased from James R. Williamson & Son, Workington for £750 each, for that purpose.

44 The 'Tobacco Pipes'. Tobacco which had been damaged in transit or had been seized by customs officers was destroyed in a specially built furnace situated on high land between Whitehaven and Parton. Whitehaven was a leading tobacco port until *c.*1760, and the tobacco pipes had been disused for over a century when they were demolished in 1923.

45 A view of the Harbour from the Prospect.

46 Whitehaven piers. The nearest is the Old New Quay with the West Pier behind it. On the right is the lighthouse on North Pier.

47   The old harbour offices after the installation of the clock, *c*.1894.

By and large the Harbour property was found to be in good structural order and very little work needed to be carried out. Unfortunately, there was a serious storm in December 1894, which damaged the West Pier, the Lime Tongue, the Sugar Tongue and the harbour offices. It was also found that the hurries were blocked, and that the Harbour's weighbridge was inaccurate. Sabotage was considered a possible cause of the last two problems.

The commissioners raised the height of the tower on the harbour offices in 1895. Their share of the cost was £25. They also improved the water supply to West Pier as the existing supply was inadequate for the use of the cattle imported from the Isle of Man and Ireland.

Exposure to harsh weather, and constant use over many years caused damage to several buildings, which resulted in their demolition. The coal hurries, after some 80 years of heavy usage, were demolished shortly after the end of the First World War. The shed on the Sugar Tongue had to be partially demolished in 1929, as it was becoming unsafe. The remaining part was destroyed by fire in 1947. The harbour offices, built in 1876, were demolished in 1956, as the foundations on the Harbour side had begun to subside.

48   The shed on the Sugar Tongue shortly before demolition. The cast-iron stanchions can be clearly seen.

The Harbour Commissioners

The last meeting of the Trustees of the Town and Harbour was held on 6 November 1894, and elections were held shortly afterwards for the new town council and also for Harbour Commissioners to represent the traders and shipowners, and the bondholders. In his capacity as Lord of the Manor of St Bees, Hugh Cecil, 5th Earl of Lonsdale, nominated a deputy and three commissioners. The full Board of Commissioners was as follows:

HUGH CECIL 5TH EARL OF LONSDALE

LONSDALE'S DEPUTY

| William Little | Hutton Hall, Penrith | Gentleman |

LONSDALE'S NOMINEES

James Robert Bain	Moresby Hall	Whitehaven Colliery
Henry Kitchin	St Bees	Druggist
Wilfred White	Whitehaven	Accountant

THE TOWN COUNCIL'S NOMINEES

| Hamilton Dixon | Royal Standard PH | Wines/SpiritsMerchant |

Archibald Kitchin	Whitehaven	
Jonathan Cant	160 Queen Street	Gentleman
Thomas K Metcalfe	9 Oakbank	Grocer

ELECTED BY THE TRADERS AND SHIPOWNERS

John Jackson	Hensingham House	Trader &Shipowner
Thomas Johnstone Black	38 Lowther Street	Coal Merchant
James Baird	10 Corkickle	Iron Ore Merchant

ELECTED BY THE BONDHOLDERS

Thomas Howson	143 Queen Street	Solicitor
Thomas Atkinson	Sea View Bransty	Gentleman
Wilson Fell Hunter	5 Roper Street	Druggist
Ralph Carr	1 Albion Terrace	Pawnbroker

John Jackson was elected chairman, and the first meeting of the new Board took place in the Town Hall on 16 November 1894.

The Board took over all the officers of the old Trust except for the treasurer, to which position they appointed Thomas Machell, the manager of Whitehaven Joint Stock Bank. John Tyson, solicitor, was appointed clerk and secretary at a salary of £125 per annum. He was required to be in his office from 10 a.m. until 5 p.m. daily. The Board appointed Brockbank, Helder and Brockbank as their solicitors, and Andrew Reed C.A. and Wilson Franks C.A. as their auditors. Reed and Franks received an annual retainer of six guineas each.

The Board arranged to meet on the first Friday of each month in the Town Hall, and also on every Friday in the harbour offices. After the sale of the Town Hall, all meetings were held in the harbour offices.

Three committees of the Board were created: the finance, the works and the general purposes committees. Early decisions were taken not to insure certain plant, including two new hoppers which cost together £1,500. However, all the Board's employees were insured under the Workmen's Compensation Act (1880). The Board was, of course, in a very difficult financial position, as all the debts of the Harbour had been taken over. However, by March 1895, it was possible to place the sum of £1,000 on deposit, as they were required to do by previous arrangement with the bondholders.

The Commissioners were keen to institute and enforce the bye-laws of the Harbour. In May 1895, it was decided that bathing from the piers was to be banned after 9 a.m. on any day. Two boys were caught throwing stones into the Harbour. At first, steps were taken to prosecute them, but they were eventually let off with a reprimand.

Among significant works carried out by the Commissioners was the renewal of the dock gates in the 1920s. During the Second World War, the patent slip went out of use and the swing bridge was fixed in position for use only by the railway. The bridge was eventually dismantled shortly after the war.

49 The dredger *Clearway* as purchased by the Harbour Commission in 1928. Although her steam crane was replaced by a diesel powered one, she was propelled by a steam driven screw until withdrawn from service in 1993.

Over a period of 100 years, the Board of Commissioners has been responsible for the maintenance, operation and administration of Whitehaven Harbour. Despite many difficulties these tasks have been carried out successfully, and the present Commissioners continue to perform these duties.

At the time of writing (December 1993) the Board of Commissioners consists of:

The Lord of the Manor of St Bees—James, 7th Earl of Lonsdale

LORD LONSDALE'S DEPUTY
The Hon. J.N. Lowther

COPELAND BOROUGH COUNCIL'S NOMINEES
Mrs. M.E. Stalker
Mr. O.J. Coyles
Mr. R. Gill
Mr. H. Wormstup

ELECTED BY THE TRADERS AND SHIPOWNERS
Mr. J.R. Gilmartin
Mr. W.C. Madine M.B.E.
One Vacancy

ELECTED BY THE BONDHOLDERS
Mrs. C. Jepson
Mr. R. Moore
Mr. A.E.H. Salvesen
Mr. J.H. Markham
Mr. Thomson is chairman and Mr. Gilmartin, vice-chairman.
The General Manager and Clerk to the Commissioners is Mr. R. Rigg.

In 1894, it was made clear that women could not even stand for election as commissioners, let alone take their seats. This was the position until 1991, when it was altered by a Harbour Revision Order.

Trade through the Harbour

At the beginning of the 20th century, the export of coal was still the mainstay of the economic life of Whitehaven Harbour. Direct control of the Whitehaven collieries by the Lowthers had come to an end in 1888. The profits of the coal mines had been falling drastically and rapidly over the immediately preceding years, apparently largely because of a series of fraudulent dealings by employees which resulted in the prosecution and imprisonment of several of them.

The collieries and their ancillaries were leased to the Whitehaven Colliery Company. The shareholders of this company were Sir James Bain, his sons, Colonel J.R. Bain and Mr. J.D. Bain, and Mr. J.S. Simpson. The property leased consisted of Henry, William, Wellington, Croft James, Duke, Saltom and Kells pits with their equipment, together with 72 coke ovens and 578 cottages. For the pits, including a sub-lease of St Bees School coal, the certain annual rent was £10,000, plus £3,000 for the fixed plant and coke ovens, and £1,014 for 139 of the cottages. After five years an additional rent became payable in respect of the remaining 439 cottages. In addition a dead rent of 8d. per ton was payable on all coal when selling price was below 9s. per ton. When above 9s., one tenth of the excess was to be added to the royalty.

Bain also controlled collieries and ironworks at Harrington, and owned a fleet of steamers sailing to ports in Ireland. The Whitehaven Colliery Company was very successful for a period of some 25 years. In 1913, however, only one of the shareholders was still alive. No exploratory work had been carried out in the mines for many years, and only the main band of coal was being worked, producing 518,000 tons a year. The lease was due to expire in 1919 and it was therefore decided to form a limited liability company. The Whitehaven Colliery Company Limited, consisting chiefly of local businessmen, took over the lease to continue the collieries.

Ever increasing quantities of locally-mined coal were being converted into coke for use in the iron and steel industries. In 1907, only 17 per cent of Cumberland mined coal was converted into coke. By 1914, this had increased to 40 per cent, or some

Haig Colliery, Whitehaven. The scene of the Great disaster whereby 39 men lost their lives on Sept. 5th, 1922.
Benton, 37, Church Lane, Hull.

50   Haig Pit.

936,000 tons. Coal output in the county had risen from 1,490,000 tons in 1866, to 2,133,000 tons in 1912. However, the industry was in severe recession after 1873. Profitability fell steadily over many years and, although output was increasing, productivity fell dramatically. For several reasons, most of which led to high absenteeism and many strikes, Cumberland had the lowest output per man shift of the coalfields in Britain. It was obviously better for the mine owners to lease their pits than to rely on their profitability. Many pits were transferred to iron-masters as part of the vertical integration of their industry. For them it was better to own the coal mines than to rely on the coal owners.

In addition to coke production, large quantities of coal were used to manufacture tar, benzol and sulphate of ammonia. Consequently, only a comparatively small proportion of the total amounts of coal mined was available for shipment by sea. Very large tonnages were moved by rail to other parts of Britain.

Ireland was still Whitehaven's principal market for coal. At the beginning of the Second World War, some 250,000 tons of coal were exported through Whitehaven Harbour. However, this was only a small fraction of Ireland's total imports, competition being very severe from the Scottish and Lancashire coalfields. During the war, large tonnages of coal were despatched from the north-east coalfields to the Irish market. Some of this was moved by rail to Maryport, and some to Barrow, and thence to Ireland. What had started as a war measure to protect the shipping from enemy attack continued until 1953. Coal movements from Whitehaven were also affected by the imposition of an import duty of 5s. per ton, levied by the Irish Government from 1932 to 1935. In addition, the development of the Prince of Wales Dock at Workington had a dramatic effect, not only on Whitehaven, but to an even greater extent on Maryport. Shipments from both ports declined dramatically.

In 1933 the Whitehaven Colliery Co. Ltd. was served with a writ by the landlord to repossess the property. The company was accused of 'having adopted a lamentably weak general policy', and besides, Whitehaven coal was becoming increasingly difficult to sell because of the decline in quality which resulted from inefficient grading and screening plant, and the lease was taken over by Priestman Whitehaven Collieries Limited for a term of 98 years at a certain rent of £10,000 with a further rent of £3,581 per annum for the farms and cottages. Following considerable investment and re-organisation, Priestman's succeeded in reviving the flagging company for a short time, but despite strenuous efforts, the company had to close in October 1935. This was a severe blow to the Cumberland coalfield and particularly to the town and harbour of Whitehaven, both of which relied so heavily on the coal industry.

Whitehaven Collieries were taken over the Cumberland Coal Company (Whitehaven) Ltd. and the mines were re-opened in March 1937. The controlling interest in this company was held by the Coltness Iron Company. During the Second World War approximately one third of the coal mined in Cumberland was mined at Whitehaven. About one quarter of the output was despatched via the Harbour, to the Isle of Man and Northern Ireland. By this time tonnages to the Irish Free State were much reduced although still significant.

Shipped tonnages continued at about 200,000 per annum until 1959. Ten years later, exports had fallen to 100,000 tons, and the decline continued until January 1982, when the last coal shipments were made from Whitehaven. During the last few years some of the coal came from the open-cast dispersal unit at Maryport.

Beacon Mills

Mr. John Pattinson, in partnership with Mr. H.C. Pattinson and Mr. H. Winter, came to Whitehaven in 1885, and established a corn business in Barracks Mill, Catherine Street. The partnership owned three steamships, *Margaret*, *Clint* and *Busk*, which were employed to bring grain from Liverpool to Whitehaven. In 1907, Pattinson built the Beacon Mills on the old shipbuilding site on North Shore. In 1949, the business was sold to Quaker Oats Ltd., but consumer demand changed and the company closed in 1972. Beacon Mills, a magnificent brick structure, was demolished in 1975. Quantities of oats were imported into Whitehaven over many years. In the 1950s the amount was about 12,500 tons per annum. Mr. Pattinson served for two terms as Mayor of Whitehaven, 1896/7 and 1897/8.

51 Pattinson's Beacon Mills.

Marchon Products Ltd.

During the Second World War, Marchon Products Ltd. moved to a site at Kells and began the manufacture of toiletry chemicals and, later, heavy duty detergent powders. The decision was also taken to manufacture sodium tripolyphosphate, an essential ingredient in detergents. This requires phosphoric acid which is produced by reacting sulphuric acid with calcium phosphate (better known as phosphate rock). The phosphate rock was imported from Casablanca, initially in chartered ships, but later in Marchon's own vessels, the *Marchon Trader*, the *Marchon Enterprise* and the *Marchon Venturer*. Imports began in 1954, and continued until 1965, when it became clear that the harbour facilities needed to be enlarged. An extensive harbour development scheme was prepared, but it did not materialise. However, two large concrete silos, fed by a system of conveyors, were built alongside Queen's Dock and behind Tangier Street. From the large vessels which anchored outside the harbour, the phosphate rock was then transferred to Queen's Dock using the specially-built barge the *Odin*. Many millions of tons of phosphate rock were imported successfully using this system until 1992 when it was decided to import the phosphoric acid in liquid form through Workington Harbour, which already had the necessary facilities.

In addition, aluminium ingots for High Duty Alloys, Distington, were imported through Whitehaven, as well as quantities of timber.

The Future

At the end of 1993, although Whitehaven Harbour was still a working harbour, activity was at a low level. The Commissioners and their General Manager, however, are of the opinion that the Harbour has a sound commercial future. The Harbour is now seen as an element in the regeneration of the town and harbour, with the aim of attracting visitors to the area, particularly from the nearby Lake District.

One company, the Whitehaven Development Company, has been established as a vehicle for directing the joint resources and expertise of Copeland Borough Council, West Cumbria Development Agency and English Estates to promote the regeneration of Whitehaven. The renaissance of Whitehaven Harbour will, it is thought, boost the town's flagging economy, provide new jobs, and really put Whitehaven on the map as a tourist, visitor and service centre.

A scheme, published in autumn 1993, envisages:

(1)   The development of a crescent of land surrounding the Harbour, which would include the provision of new houses, offices, retail space, commercial floor space, and tourist facilities (restaurants etc.). It is suggested that these developments could create about 1,800 new jobs.

(2)   The pedestrianisation of certain areas in the town centre, the recreation of Williamson Lane, Mark Lane, and the improvement of Lower Duke Street and Lower Lowther Street.

(3)   The re-routing of motor traffic through the town centre.

These developments, it is said, would improve the attractiveness of the town, for the benefit of both the local people and also for visitors.

This scheme, of course, has met with mixed reactions. The total scheme will take ten years to complete, and it will cost several million pounds.

Sources

The Minute Books of the Whitehaven Harbour Commissioners.
Fancy, H., *Around Whitehaven in Old Photographs* (1992).
Hay, D., *An Illustrated History of Whitehaven* (1979).
Owen, C.H.H., *The Lowther Family* (1990).
Wood, O., *West Cumberland Coal 1600-1982/3* (1988).
Whitehaven Development Company (1993).

Appendix A

Plans for Improvement

In 1836 the Trustees of Whitehaven Town and Harbour published a volume of 19 plans of proposed improvements to the harbour. Measuring 18" x 14¼". This very scarce book commences with a report by the eminent civil engineer John Smeaton, following his visit to survey the harbour in 1768. Plan I shows the harbour as it was in 1792. The other plans show various proposals for extending or improving the harbour submitted between 1804 and 1836. The majority, with notes by the proposers, were never implemented. A small selection of these plans, with comments, is reproduced on a much smaller scale, by kind permission of Whitehaven Museum. It is interesting to note that the outstanding engineers John Rennie and his more famous son Sir John were both responsible for major phases in the development of the harbour during the 19th century (see plans dated 1823 and 1834).

WHITEHAVEN HARBOUR.

The REPORT of JOHN SMEATON, Engineer, upon a View of the Harbour of Whitehaven.

Having carefully viewed the Harbour of Whitehaven upon the 7th and 8th of April, 1768, I am of opinion as follows :—

That in case the Expense and length of Time attending such a Work would permit its Execution, that the noblest and best Scheme would be to carry out a North Pier, and to lengthen the New Pier, till the Heads of the Two Piers should be within a competent distance (suppose Two Hundred Feet) of each other; but as I apprehend it would be many years before much Relief could be procured to the trade by so extensive a Work, the most ready way of enlarging the Harbour would be by extending the Old Pier by some additional Works, the Particulars of which it will require leisure to judge of; but I am clearly of Opinion, that if, during the coming Summer, the Old Pier can be lengthened Thirty Yards, and turned a little more Outward than the present Direction, it will perfectly agree with every just idea of what is to follow, and that the Prolongation aforesaid should be the first Work done; and if during this Time a correct Plan of the Harbour, Piers, and Appurtenances, together with the Coast as far as Redness Point, is prepared to be laid before me, I shall then be in a condition to judge more accurately of what is to follow.

JOHN SMEATON.

Cockermouth, 8th April, 1768.

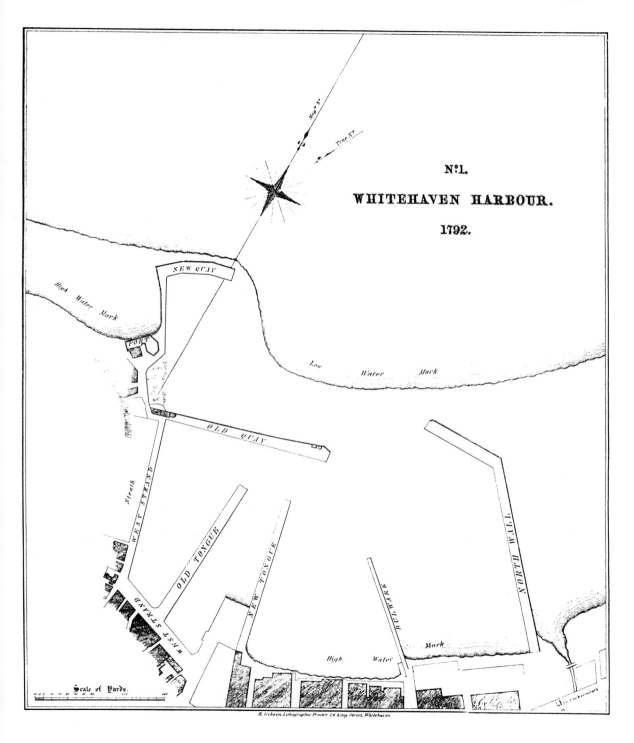

NO. 1.

WHITEHAVEN HARBOUR.

1792.

WHITEHAVEN HARBOUR.

The REPORT of J. HUDDART, Hydrographer, accompanied by a PLAN for the Improvement of Whitehaven Harbour.

TO ROBERT BLAKENEY, ESQUIRE.

Dear Sir,—I have received your favour of the 28th ultimo, inclosing a Plan and suggested Improvement for the Northern Part of the Harbour of Whitehaven, requesting my further Consideration of this Subject at the Request of the Trustees.

I was desirous to view the Harbour in its present State (in order to ascertain whether the Effect of the late Works were what I had reason to expect) before I gave an Opinion upon the Tongue or Breakwater, for Stilling the North Harbour, which I have done; and taking the whole into Consideration, I give it as my Opinion, that the North Tongue should begin at the Right Line, joining the Extremities of the New Quay, and the North Pier or Quay continued, leaving Thirty Eight Yards clear, *A c*, between the North Quay and the Tongue, at its South West Angle. From which Point the Tongue to be extended in a Right Line, *A B*, to join the Old Bulwark at Fifty Yards distance from the South West Angle of the Sugar House Yard, as by the Inclosed Plan; in which the North Tongue (with an additional Breadth to the Bulwark) is coloured Red, and which additional Breadth may be further extended down the Tongue as occasion may require for Business.

I have mentioned Thirty Eight Yards of clear opening for better Accommodation, presuming that the North Harbour will then be so still as not to occasion any Damage to the Shipping therein; but if a further Reduction of Waves is thought necessary, it may be obtained by adding to the length of the Tongue as represented by Dotted Lines, *A b*, at any future Period.

It is also my Opinion that this Tongue will not sensibly effect the Old Harbour, and will render the whole Area of the North Harbour perfectly secure for Shipping.

I am, Sir,

Your most Obedient,

J. HUDDART.

Allonby, 27th October, 1804.

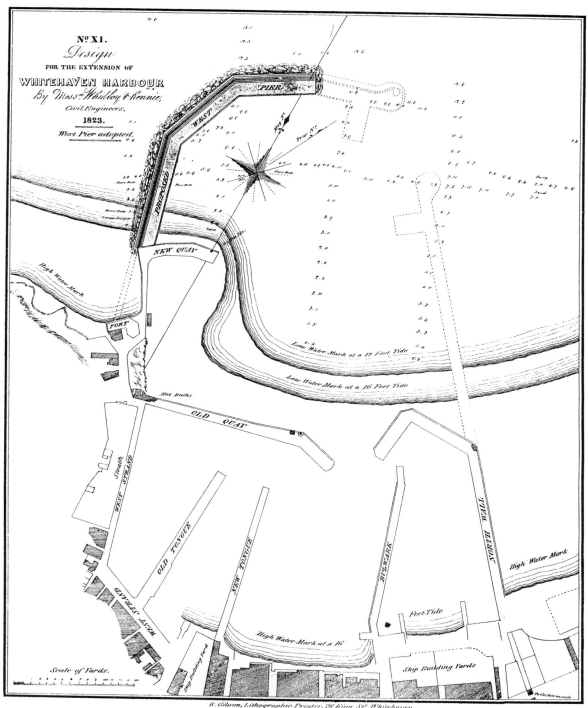

WHITEHAVEN HARBOUR.

Report of Messrs. WHIDBEY and RENNIE on the Means of Improving the Harbour of Whitehaven.

London, May 30, 1823.

Gentlemen,—In consequence of the Directions communicated to us through your late Secretary, Mr. Blakeney, we proceeded to Whitehaven in the Month of October last, for the purpose of Inspecting the Harbour, and reporting our Opinion upon the most advisable Measures to be adopted for improving it and rendering it more serene for large Ships at all times of Tide. The Inconveniences of the present Harbour have been so long felt, and so ably and repeatedly discussed by others, that it would be needless further to enlarge upon them here; it may suffice to observe that the present Evils are universally admitted and imperiously call for a remedy.

To obviate the Two principal Evils, namely, want of a sufficient Depth at Low Water of Spring Tides, and the insecurity during Storms from the principal obnoxious Winds, namely, the West and North West, we propose to run out a New Pier from the New Quay, and in the direction laid down upon the accompanying Plan, having its Head terminating in a Depth of nearly Eight Feet Six Inches at Low Water of an extraordinary Spring Tide, which took place on the 31st of December last, and rose Twenty-four Feet Six Inches above Low Water of the same Tide; such a Depth of Water, during such high Tides, would in our Opinion afford ample Accommodation for the largest Class of Vessels that are ever likely to visit this part of the Island. The principal object we have in view is to obtain as much Water as possible at Low Water, at the proposed Pier Head, and also to make the Water smooth within it, so that Ships may enter with Ease and Safety within the Pier at an early part of the Tide. This we conceive will be the case when the Pier is finished, and we hope that by erecting such a Pier all the Expectations of the Trustees of the Harbour of Whitehaven will be accomplished, without going to a prodigious Expense by extending the Pier further Westward, and placing the Head of it in Thirteen Feet at Low Water of Spring Tide, and extending it on towards Tom Herd's Rock.

The Direction of the proposed Pier and Entrance is similar to that designed by the late Mr. Rennie, which under all Circumstances we are of Opinion is best adapted for Whitehaven. The grand Objection to having the Entrance so far to the Northward, namely, that Vessels entering during heavy Gales of Wind from the exposed Quarters would be liable to be driven on the Beach on the Northern Side of the Bay, is in our Opinion Groundless, inasmuch as they would have ample Room to bring up under the shelter of the proposed New Pier, independent of the Eddy Current within the Bay, which would effectually prevent them from driving to Leeward.

For the present we merely propose to carry into Execution the Pier as delineated on the Drawing, leaving the Extension of the Northern Pier, with its Jetty and the Jetty for the Western Pier, in the manner proposed by the late Mr. Rennie, to be executed in Proportion as Circumstances may require. We have run out the New Pier, in the first Instance, nearly at Right Angles to the New Quay, in order that if at any future Period a Wet Dock, or further Improvements may be required, as suggested by the late Mr. Rennie, they may be obtained by extending the Wall in the Direction marked by the dotted Lines towards the Half Moon Battery. In that case the straight Wall from the Fort to the Departure of the First Kant of the proposed New Pier would form a Division by which the remaining Space would be converted into a spacious Wet Basin, or any other Purpose that might be required.

The Estimates, £67,274, are founded upon Information derived at Whitehaven, which added to the fall of Materials since the Year 1814, has made a considerable Difference in favour of the present Time. When the great Pier proposed has been carried into Execution, the beneficial Consequences resulting from it to the Trade of Whitehaven will be most Important, and the Trustees will be amply Remunerated for the Expense of carrying it into Execution.

We are,

Gentlemen,

Your very humble Servants,

JOHN WHIDBEY,
JOHN RENNIE.

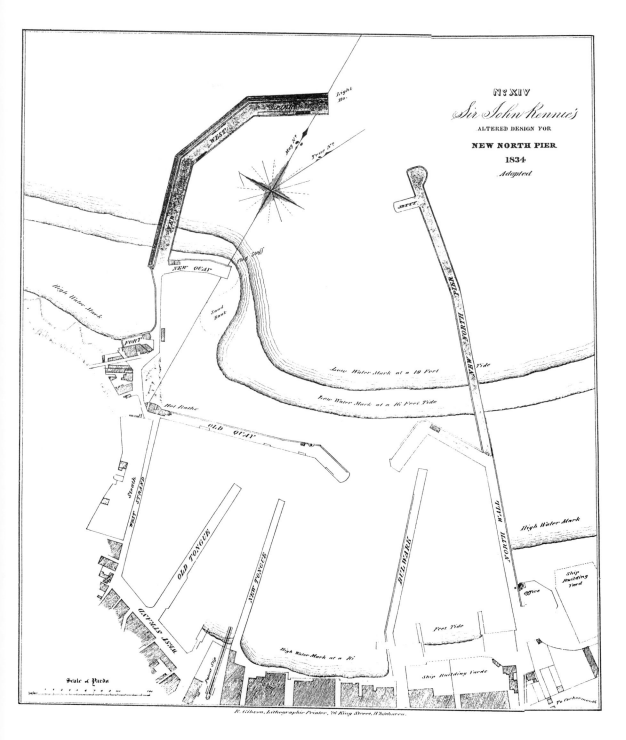

Nº XIV

Sir John Rennie's

ALTERED DESIGN FOR

NEW NORTH PIER

1834

Adopted

F. Gibson, Lithographic Printer, 26 King Street, Whitehaven.

WHITEHAVEN HARBOUR.

Proposed Alteration in the Direction of the New North Pier.

London, 27th March, 1834.

Gentlemen,—In consequence of your Resolution of the 1st of January last, requesting me to consider whether it is advisable to make any Alteration in the Direction of the New North Pier, I have done so accordingly; but previously to entering upon this Question it is right to Determine how the West Pier should be finished also, for upon this the Plan for completing the North Pier materially depends.

Upon the Propriety of continuing the West Pier further there are various Opinions; some consider that it is sufficiently advanced to the North, while others are of Opinion that it is not far enough. Taking into Consideration however all the Reasons adduced on both Sides, I think that upon the whole a little further Addition will be advisable.

First,—Because during severe Westerly Gales a heavy Swell accompanied by broken Water, sets past the present Head, and renders it difficult for Vessels to steer properly whilst passing it. By extending this Head about Thirty-two Yards further, and making it Circular, the Sea will be diverted, and the Inconvenience will be avoided.

Secondly,—Because it will give more Shelter to the Mouth of the Inner Harbour.

In addition to extending the Pier Head as above mentioned, it is not improbable but that a Jetty at Right Angles to it may be required, as shewn on the Drawing, but this, together with the other may be deferred until after the North Pier has been completed.

The above point being determined, the next Question is, how should the North Pier be finished?

Upon this it may be observed that inasmuch at the heaviest Sea comes from the Westward, and might otherwise enter the Harbour, I am decidedly of Opinion that the North Pier should terminate rather within the West Pier Head. This, however must not be carried too far.

First,—Because Vessels at times might find some difficulty in entering.

Secondly,—The Current out of the Harbour would be too directly opposed to the Counter Current in the Bay, and consequently might tend to produce a Shoal or Bar at the Harbour Mouth, which would be very Inconvenient.

Thirdly,—The Outer Harbour would be contracted without diminishing the Expense.

Upon these principles the Harbour Mouth has been already designed, and I should recommend them to be adhered to; and by pursuing them further the Plan may be improved and the Harbour rendered still more Tranquil, viz., by inclining the Outer Part of the Pier towards the Main Arm, and by making a Jetty at Right Angles to it, about One Hundred Feet long, upon the Principle of the late Mr. Rennie, and still leaving an entrance of near Two Hundred and Forty Feet wide between the Outer Pier Heads.

This would not increase the Estimate, or occasion any Alteration in the Work already finished, and would render the Interior of the Harbour more Tranquil, and the North Pier more serviceable for Ships to lie alongside when completed. I have therefore prepared the accompanying Plan and recommend it to be adopted accordingly.

The next Point to be considered is, how the Inconvenience which is produced by the Accumulation of the Swell along the Inside Wall of the North Pier may be avoided during its Construction. This it is true, is Inconvenient, although only of a temporary Nature. To obviate it, therefore, that part of the Work which has already been commenced near the Old North Wall should not be raised higher at present, and the Outer Part of the Main Arm, as well as the Pier Head and Kant, should be founded and carried up first. These will then form a Protection for the Interior Harbour; and in the mean time the other End of the Pier, by being kept at its present Level will permit any Waves which may enter, and otherwise Accumulate along the Front Wall, to escape, without producing any Swell; and, if necessary, this may be promoted still further, by constructing a temporary Carcase of Wood, according to the annexed Sketch, No. 2, filled with loose Rubble, and set at Right Angles to the Pier wherever the Sea accumulates.

I also beg leave to send a Plan of a Double Crane, marked No 3, for carrying on the Work, which will, I think, be found very useful and economical, and as I shall be in constant Communication with Mr. Logan, if any thing else should occur it shall be communicated.

I beg to apologize that I have been prevented by unforeseen Circumstances from sending this before.

I am,

Gentlemen,

Your humble Servant,

JOHN RENNIE.

To the Trustees of Whitehaven Harbour, &c. &c. &c.

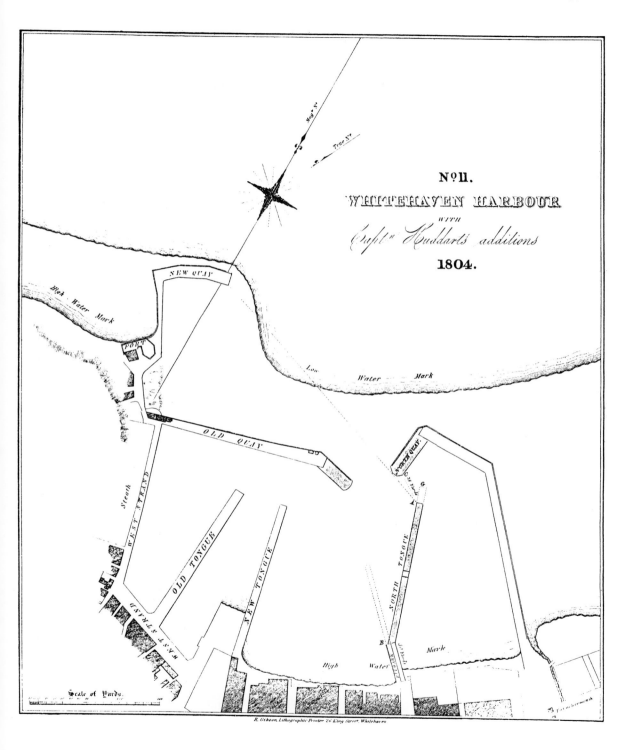

Appendix B

Owners of the Whitehaven Estates

Sir Christopher Lowther (Whitehaven) 1611-44. Created steward of the Whitehaven estates by his father, Sir John Lowther of Lowther, and inherited the estates in 1637. Created 1st Baronet of Whitehaven by Charles I in 1642. Succeeded by his son ...

Sir John Lowther (Whitehaven) 1642-1706. 2nd Baronet of Whitehaven, M.P. for Cumberland 1665-1700. Created Baron Lowther of Lowther and Viscount Lonsdale in 1697. Sir John disinherited his elder son and was succeeded by his younger son ...

Sir James Lowther (Whitehaven) 1673-1755. 4th and last Baronet of Whitehaven. M.P. for Carlisle, 1694-1702, for Cumberland, 1708-22 and 1725-55 and for Appleby, 1723-7. Bequeathed the estates to his third cousin ...

Sir William Lowther of Holker (Marske and Holker) 1727-56. 3rd and last Baronet of Holker. M.P. for Cumberland 1755-6. The estates then passed to ...

Sir James Lowther (Maulds Meaburn) 1736-1802. 5th and last Baronet of Lowther. Created 1st Earl of Lonsdale 1784. M.P. for Cumberland 1757-68 and 1774-84, for Westmorland 1761-2, and for Cockermouth 1769-74. As a result of the will of Sir James Lowther, the estates were then inherited by ...

Sir William Lowther of Swillington 1757-1844. 2nd Baronet of Swillington, 2nd Viscount Lowther. Created 1st Earl of Lonsdale 1807. M.P. for Carlisle 1784-90, for Rutland 1796-1802. Was succeeded by his son ...

William Lowther 1787-1872. Viscount Lowther from 1807. 2nd Earl of Lonsdale from 1844. M.P. for Cockermouth 1808-13, for Westmorland 1813-31, and 1832-41, and for Dunwich 1832. He was succeeded by his nephew ...

Henry Lowther 1818-76. 3rd Earl of Lonsdale. M.P. for Cumberland 1847-72. Was succeeded by his eldest son ...

St George Henry Lowther 1855-82. 4th Earl of Lonsdale. He was followed by his brother Hugh Cecil 1867-1944, 5th Earl of Lonsdale, the 'Yellow Earl', who in turn was also succeeded by a brother ...

Lancelot Edward Lowther 1867-1953. 6th Earl of Lonsdale. After his death, the estates passed to his grandson ...

James Hugh William Lowther b.1922. 7th Earl of Lonsdale.

Index

Numbers in **bold** type refer to illustration numbers

Isle of Man.   New West Pier.
                     New East Pier, now building.

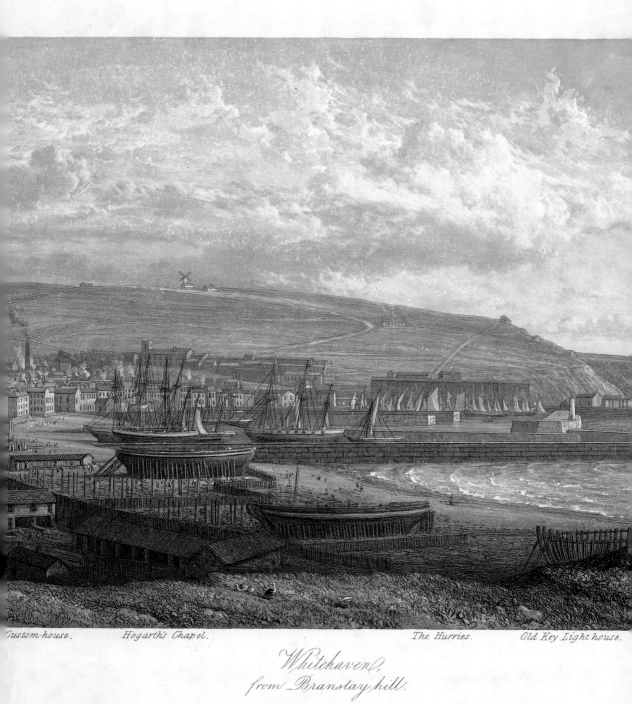

Custom-house. Hogarth's Chapel. The Hurries. Old Key Light house.

Whitehaven,
from Branstay hill.

Published by Ackermann & Cº 96 Strand. 1834.

&. Engraved by W. Westall, A.R.A.

Trinity Church.   St Nicholas Church.   Branstay Arch.